The Natural Gas Market

The Natural Gas Market

Sixty Years of Regulation

and Deregulation

Paul W. MacAvoy

Yale University Press

New Haven and London

Set in Adobe Garamond and Stone Sans type by The Composing Room of Michigan, Inc.
Printed in the United States of America.

Library of Congress Cataloging-in-Publication Data

MacAvoy, Paul W.
    The natural gas market: sixty years of regulation and deregulation / Paul W. MacAvoy.
        p.   cm.
    Includes bibliographical references and index.
    ISBN 0-300-08381-5 (cloth : alk. paper)
    1. Natural gas—Law and legislation—United States—History.   2. Deregulation—United States—History.   I. Title: The natural gas market: sixty years of regulation and deregulation.   II. Title.

KF2130 .M33   2001
343.73'0772—dc21   00-040837

A catalogue record for this book is available from the British Library.

To William E. Simon, who perceived the problem very early on: writing in 1977 in *A Time for Truth,* "It is with inexpressible indignation that I report here that while this book was being written we had our next energy crisis, a frightening shortage of natural gas in the coldest winter in 100 years. Natural gas was concentrated, of course, in those states where the free market price existed and ran short in those states where federal price controls had reduced the supply. . . . Had anything been learned at all?"

Contents

Figures

Tables

Preface

The natural gas industry over the past sixty years has provided a natural experiment in regulation's effects on the performance of suppliers in wholesale and retail markets. The different regulatory strategies that have been introduced have included cost-justified gas price ceilings, elimination of some gas price ceilings, elimination of all gas price ceilings, and voluntary and then required divestiture of gas ownership by pipeline transporters. The resulting performance included gas shortages, larger than in any other industry, during the mid-1970s, and then large gas surpluses, in what was termed the "gas bubble," in the early 1980s. The regulation that remains today has effects that currently are more difficult to determine, but indications are that the industry operates below its potential for providing gas and transportation. Most remarkable, while deregulating, federal and state regulatory agencies have become even more intrusive in the individual transactions among producer, pipeline, distributor, and consumer. The industry now does better—after all, for two decades it performed the worst of any regulated industry. But perhaps it is not performing as well as it could if the forty years of regulation, since the Natural Gas

Act of 1938, and the twenty years of partial deregulation, since the Natural Gas Policy Act of 1978, had been followed by complete deregulation.

This chronicle is developed in six chapters. It is intended to be instructive as to the generic process of regulation in not only the energy but also other regulated industries. In natural gas regulation every tool in the kit bag of the regulating authorities has been tried, in what publicly has been a quest to make the consumer better off. Nothing has "worked," in that there were no gains to consumers, nor were there gains to producers or pipelines. Attempts to implement price ceiling regulation, phased price ceiling deregulation, and vertical unbundling of services are under way in the electric and telecommunications industries. Those undertaking these efforts can take notice that they have all been found to be wanting in the natural gas industry, at least when the goal has been the enhancement of consumer welfare.

I began this work in my Yale doctoral dissertation in the last half of the 1950s, subsequently published as *Price Formation in Natural Gas Fields: A Study of Competition Monopsony and Regulation* (Yale University Press, 1962). Professor (now Justice) Stephen Breyer and I undertook an analysis of the Federal Power Commission for the Brookings Institution in the early 1970s, which led to publication of *Energy Regulation by the Federal Power Commission* (1974). Further research was undertaken while I was associated with the MIT Sloan School of Management and the MIT Energy Laboratory; this resulted in the book I co-wrote with Robert S. Pindyck, *The Economics of the Natural Gas Shortage, 1960–1980* (North-Holland Publishing, 1975). The Natural Gas Policy Act of 1978 was analyzed in an article published in the *Natural Resources Journal* (October 1979). In the early 1990s, I testified before the Federal Energy Regulatory Commission for various pipelines on their gas purchase agreements during the "bubble" period (for example, in FERC RP 85-177-122, et al., 1993) and was a member of Commissioner Branko Terzic's Task Force at FERC in 1994 on developing a framework for assessing the competitiveness of gas transportation.

During the past five years I have carried on this work on gas industry behavior and regulation with very substantial research support from the John M. Olin Foundation Research Program for the Study of Markets and Regulatory Behavior at the Yale School of Management. This program has analyzed regulatory agency behavior in a number of industries, and my research on natural gas has been part of that effort. I have had the assistance of Olin Senior Fellows Gary Davison, Jean Wallace Frazier, Victor Santini, and Nickolay V. Moshkin. I am grateful to them and to the Olin Foundation for making this book possible. Central to this work has been the counsel and assistance of Michael Doane and Michael Williams of PM Industrial Economics, whose contributions to analysis of gas industry behavior are well known. My acknowledgment of their assistance, and that of the scholars listed in the References, is extensive and indeed only limited by the necessity to take responsibility for all that is stated here. The draft manuscript was evaluated by two readers for the Yale Press; their critiques, particularly that of the distinguished emeritus professor at Pennsylvania State University, Richard L. Gordon, were of substantial assistance in revising for publication. I thank Sharon Krischtschun and Marjorie Wakefield for crafting a book out of a manuscript and Kay MacAvoy for her patience.

The Natural Gas Market

Chapter 1 An Introduction to Regulation and the Performance of Gas Markets

The price and production behavior of gas markets has been strikingly different from that in markets for other natural resources. Gas prices in constant dollars began to increase in the mid-1970s, peaked in 1982–1983, and have declined almost every year since then. Production peaked in the mid-1970s, after some years in which new discoveries of in-ground reserves failed to replace the annual take from operating wells; by the early 1980s, production had stabilized at 80 percent of peak levels, while reserves continued to decline.

Although this price spike characterized market behavior, it resulted not from supply-demand interactions but from distortions caused by the application of regulatory policies specific to the natural gas industry. The impact of regulation has been all-encompassing, on the wellhead contract commitment of reserves, on production out of reserves, and on pipeline delivery of production to the city gate for distribution to final consumers.

Federal regulatory policy in the 1960s and 1970s placed limits on gas prices that caused significant nationwide shortages, and in response, new policy in the late 1970s then caused surpluses that closed

1

down production facilities and led to dumping gas in spot markets. A Supreme Court decision of 1954 required federal regulatory control of the wellhead price of gas. It took until the late 1960s to implement this ruling at the Federal Power Commission (FPC). When controls became fully effective, prices and thus production were reduced to such an extent that shortages exceeded one quarter of total demands. To relieve these shortages, prices were deregulated, but only for production from newly developed reserves. By continuing the regulation of prices for production out of old reserves for seven more years, the commission forced deregulated prices for new supplies to such artificially high levels that supplies exceeded demands by the mid-1980s.

These policies were intended to improve industry performance. The purpose of regulation, underlying the commission's massive proceedings on case decisions and rulemaking, was to make consumers better off, by keeping prices at the low levels realized in the 1950s and 1960s, while still making it possible for producers to make adequate returns on investment in new reserves. Regulation meant to ensure the security of supply of gas reserves for production under pipeline contracts that extended from ten to twenty years in the future.

The FPC required contracts between the gas producer and pipeline buyer that would generate sufficient supply for the pipeline buyer to meet retail utility demands for gas at low cost over the lifetimes of installed lines. The requirement was to secure price and gas throughput against the vagaries of weather, the business cycle, and unexpected increases in user demands. But actual implementation of regulatory controls froze prices for long periods, generating supply volumes that were too limited to be secure. In fact, supply volumes were so low under price caps and later so high under partial deregulation that market-pricing processes were severely disrupted.

How could we explain results that deviate so far from the straightforward goal of a secure low-cost supply? They could have been intentional, as regulators sought to favor special interests with, for example, low prices, rather than improve the security of supply for all market participants. This argument would be plausible if some interest group turns out to have substantially benefited from the disorientation of markets caused by regulation. To assess regulation-induced gains or losses for all the major participant groups in gas markets, I develop, in the following chapters, estimates of prices and quantities with and without regulation. The "with regulation" prices reflect the historical prices on actual transactions. The "without regulation" prices are from a market model of the industry at the wellhead level that determines the sequence of supply-demand equilibrium prices from year to year for the past three decades. This model is developed in Chapter 2 to simulate market-clearing behavior over the period 1970 to 1995. In Chapters 3 and 4, I analyze three major regulatory regimes by examining differences in each regime between actual prices and volumes and the model market clearing prices and volumes. Gains or losses are estimated from price differences, for consumers and any interest group, and from quantity differences as the consumer or that interest group obtains more or less gas production.

INTRODUCING THE NATURAL GAS INDUSTRY

From wells deep into the earth's surface, companies extract a hydrocarbon derivative consisting mostly of methane mixtures, which is then refined to pure methane and transported as "pipeline quality gas" to be distributed to households, commercial establishments, and industry as heating fuel or chemical product raw material. The methane mixture comes from reservoirs containing crude oils, carbon dioxide, water, and other noncommercial substances. Pure methane is extracted from the other materials for injection (at a heating value of approximately 1010 Btu per cubic foot) into local and long-distance pipelines for delivery to wholesale or final customers.

The process begins with determination of the presence of in-ground deposits of methane and other hydrocarbons by drilling discovery wells into gas-bearing rock and sands. Seismic records are used to locate likely producing formations, a technique that has advanced over the past half century from crudely indicating various formations to, in the 1990s, actually detecting gas in these formations from three-dimensional databased simulations. As knowledge of the location of concentrated gas deposits (reserves) has developed, the drilling of producing wells has been made more exact and the recovery of a high percentage of in-ground volumes has been made more probable.

Large basins of reserves in North America have been located in Texas, Louisiana, and Oklahoma; more recent finds with improved technologies have added basins in Alberta, Colorado, and New Mexico. Markets for gas production have been located in the population and industrial centers of the East Coast, the Mid-Atlantic, and the West Coast. With major reserve basins historically in the Southwest, and concentrations of consumers in the coastal regions, the key step in industry development has been the construction of large-scale gas transmission and distribution systems. The rapid and successful growth of large transmission pipelines has made it possible for the industry to become the source of more than one-quarter of U.S. primary energy consumption.

In the system that was in place from the 1930s to the mid-1980s, transmission companies, which by and large have been separate from production and distribution companies over the past fifty years, purchased gas at the wellhead to transport and sell to local distribution companies, which then sold the gas to final consumers. The purchase at the wellhead established the "field price" of the product; the pipeline-delivered gas at the city gate was resold at the "city gate price"; that gas was finally resold again by the local distributing company at the "burner tip price."

This transaction demarcation has never been absolute. Gas at times has been gathered at the wellhead for transportation to the processing plant by field producers and sold there by the plant operator to the pipeline. At other times transmission companies have owned the processing plant or themselves have been owned and operated by local distribution companies, particularly if the local distribution company was in a gas-producing region. Transmission companies have sold gas directly to large industrial consumers, in what were retail transactions, without involving local distribution companies.

This rather straightforward industry structure, built around wellhead and city gate transactions, changed entirely in the 1990s. Field production was no longer sold at the wellhead or processing plant to pipeline companies that transport the gas long distances to population or industrial centers. New federal regulations removed the pipeline from the buying side of wellhead markets, to be replaced by brokers as well as wholesale and end-use customers. The new buyers sought transportation separately from the pipeline companies to complete delivery of their product at the wellhead to the city gate. Under the cloak of partial "deregulation," regulators no longer allowed pipelines to provide a package of gas plus transportation service, and instead they required open access to pipeline space for distributors and consumers.

In effect, entirely new markets developed at various intersection points, or "hubs," in pipeline systems for gas and for pipeline space to the next intersection point. Markets also developed for in-ground storage space, to allow gas delivered off-season to be used to meet peak heating season demands at some population center close by. Secondary markets for transportation quickly developed, in which buyers of pipeline space resell excess space, in competition with pipelines offering primary contract space. New contracts developed for hedging both gas and pipeline space agreements in commodity exchange contract markets.

In any broad survey of these original and newer markets there is the threshold issue of explaining industry price and production behavior. The issue is whether natural gas, a resource in reserve deposits, has been "running out," that is, becoming more scarce as reduced results from the reserve discovery process leads to systemic price increases and production declines. Natural gas reserves declined by 35 percent in the 1970s, but then by only 3 percent in the 1980s, while production in the two periods declined by 8 and 4 percent, respectively (fig. 1.1). Reserves declined again by 3 percent in the first half of the 1990s, but production increased by 5 percent. Thus, since 1988 a smaller reserve stock has supported a higher rate of production.

If depletion has set in, then wellhead transaction prices would have had to systematically follow a certain path over time. As developed by Harold Hotelling in 1931, in the depletion phase of a natural resource, current price equals the present value of expected future price net of any difference in extraction costs; that is, prices increase in percentage terms by the rate of interest. In 1978, Robert S. Pindyck developed this relationship more fully by indicating that price increases equal the difference between the rate of interest and changes in the costs of extraction, so that if technology reduces costs, then price changes can be negative. These price increases or decreases follow from moving supply up or down the demand function; in the Hotelling case, as price increases then production declines, but in the Pindyck case the secular price declines take place as production increases.

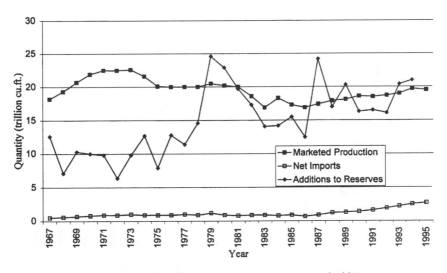

Figure 1.1. Domestic U.S. marketed gas production, net imports, and additions to gas reserves; *source:* DOE/EIA 1996, tables 4.5, 4.6, 4.10, 6.2, 6.3, app. D-1

Prices for 1970–1996 follow a pattern different from that in depletion in a natural resource industry. Rather, it is an inverted "U," with a fifteen-year period of increase and a fifteen-year period of decline (fig. 1.2). The lowest price, for gas to the pipeline at the wellhead, did not increase in constant dollar terms before 1973, but at that point and continuing to 1978, it increased at an annual rate of more than 33 percent. Production increased each year to 1974, then fell back to 1968 levels for the rest of the period. From 1978 until 1983, prices at the wellhead continued to increase at approximately 10 percent per annum, while production held constant and then fell off 10 percent. From 1983 to 1996 prices declined by approximately 5 percent per annum, to return to 1980 levels, and production increased slightly, also to return to 1980 levels.

The annual price increase after 1975 was less than the increase in the rate of interest every year, and the rate of interest explains less than half of the year-to-year variance in prices. If we separate the thirty years into three time periods associated with three regulatory regimes, any trend in prices becomes insignificant. But the first regulatory ("price ceiling") period realized a substantial increase in the price level, the second ("phased partial deregulation") period also had increases in the price level, and the third ("restructuring") period had reduced prices.

At this stage of the analysis the conclusion is that year-to-year changes in prices have not followed the pattern of any industry subject to depletion of nat-

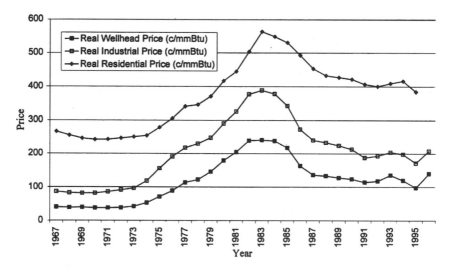

Figure 1.2. Real wellhead, industrial, and residential prices; *source:* DOE/EIA 1996, tables 6.8, 6.9, apps. A-4, D-1

ural resources. Instead, each of the three periods of price change has been associated with a different regime of regulatory controls. The first two periods were marked by controls designed to contain rising prices, and prices increased while quantities decreased. The last period, after wellhead price controls had been eliminated and wellhead purchases had been unbundled from transportation, was marked by significant price decreases but continued quantity decreases.

INTRODUCING REGULATION

In the depths of the late 1930s economy-wide depression, the Federal Power Commission began operations as a regulatory agency with statute authority to regulate the performance of electric power and natural gas companies "affected with a public interest." The Federal Power Act of 1935 assigned the commission the task of "assuring an abundant supply of electric energy throughout the United States with the greatest possible economy and with regard to the proper utilization and conservation of natural resources." The Natural Gas Act of 1938 brought under regulation companies in interstate commerce that undertook sales of gas for resale that were "affected with a public interest." Both statutes required the regulator to apply controls that would result in these companies better serving consumers. The commission was to secure "just and reasonable" prices for buyers of gas in wholesale markets to be passed on to household and business consumers.[1]

The natural gas companies regulated by the commission turned out to include not only pipelines but also producers with gas for sale at the wellhead to be transported to the city gate across state lines. For forty years, FPC decisions and reviews of those decisions by the federal courts were based on the presumption that the intent was to protect consumer interests.[2] To achieve "reasonable" prices, at the wellhead the commission required producers to sell gas at prices no greater than the average historical cost of finding and production. Given that such costs included a "fair" profit, the pipeline buyer paid that for the volume of gas taken and no more.[3] Over the same forty years, the FPC regulated pipelines by licensing their provision of service and then approving rates and service offerings in the tariff under the license. New facilities for transporting gas were certified after the commission determined the adequacy of financial resources and the sufficiency of contracted gas reserves. The regulatory purpose was to ensure that the pipelines could "meet those demands which it is reasonable to assume will be made upon them."[4] To achieve "reasonable" rates, the commission approved tariff changes proposed by the pipelines as necessary to generate revenues that would cover operating costs, depreciation, interest, and a fair return to equity investment.

During the 1960s, the FPC undertook the task of establishing comprehensive regulation of the wellhead contract for gas. The commission was attempting to meet a requirement, laid down in 1954 by the Supreme Court in *Phillips Petroleum Company v. Wisconsin,* to set limits on wellhead prices of the gas-producing companies.[5] The commission's first approach resembled pipeline tariff-rate regulation put in place twenty years earlier. Rate-setting proceedings in each case provided estimates of development costs of reserves in specific producing fields; based on these data the commission set individual price ceilings on the contract gas sold at each well. Given limits on its decision-making capacities, using this procedure, the Federal Power Commission was able to complete its review of only a few contracts in the 1950s, and thousands of wellhead sales contracts were placed in suspension with deliveries at prices not subject to review. In the early 1960s, the commission cleared out this backlog, with a new approach of setting regional price ceilings on all contracts in each of the major basins. Applying "caps" across all contracts with different vintages and production rates gave the commission control of wellhead price setting by the end of the decade.

The broadening of regulation to include controls over pricing of both the producing companies and the pipelines in interstate commerce generated substantial controversy. Objections to field-price setting were based on the lack of a rationale; surely not every field price that increased or was higher than the basin ceiling was "affected with the public interest." Beyond that, what made price increases in this industry over time so different that they had to be subject to commission control? One answer was that production was not competitive, and another was that the buyer was a regulated pipeline that was not concerned with cost and just passed on any wellhead price increase in its regulated rates at the city gate. Both answers were without foundation. In any event, by the mid-1970s, the controversy was moot. Federal Power Commission regulation was so perverse that, by any definition of the "public interest," consumers were not being served and that any rationale for regulatory intervention had become wrong.[6]

THE GOALS OF REGULATION

The mission of the Federal Power Commission can be conceived of as stabilizing prices and requiring service to enhance the interests of business and residential consumers. This conception is unsophisticated politically and in practice can conflict with enhancing the gains of specific interest groups that become involved in the regulatory process. Keeping city gate prices low is consistent with constraining monopoly profits of producers and pipelines. Increasing the accessibility and reliability of service can stimulate consumer demand; to do so, so that consumers pay no more than marginal costs, would reproduce performance found in competitive markets. Such an assessment fits a framework of regulatory and antitrust law based on achieving the benefits of competition by preventing exploitation by monopolies where industry structures cannot or do not allow competition among service providers. That requires that the regulatory agency be impartial in case-by-case proceedings involving gainers and losers and that it seek to generate competitive behavior or the results from that behavior.

It is possible that these objectives did coexist at the beginning of commission activities. In the process of installing basin-wide wellhead price ceilings, buyers with established pipeline connections did receive gas at low prices, whereas other newer buyers experienced shortages and had to turn to less desirable substitutes. After widespread shortages developed in the 1970s the Congress and the FPC attempted to resolve the conflict between consumers with and without gas by allowing marginal supplies to be priced at higher levels until those prices rose above what consumers would pay. At that point consumers had all the gas demanded at those prices but would have taken more at prices that would have been lower without regulation.

At times, without acknowledgment, the commission lapsed from concern with the public into concerns with private interests. It did so by attempting to achieve political compromise; results were satisfactory when gas producers, pipeline companies, and organized gas-user interests did not complain. In some contexts, neutrality along these lines can make sense; but the conclusion that all interest groups in gas markets gained from higher or lower prices, so that the public interest was served, is unwarranted. In fact, no interest group gained from the large-scale experiments in gas and transport regulation in the 1970s and 1980s (see Chapters 3 and 4).

PROCEDURES

At the beginning the Federal Power Commission was committed to setting prices for pipelines based on costs of service. In response to company requests for the commission to certify price increases (tariff increases), procedures were established for determining "test period" costs and for a "fair" return on investment. The commission analyzed accounting measures of expenditures and revenues of the regulated companies with procedures that were intricate, detailed, and comprehensive. It made decisions based on its findings to ensure adequacy of transmission capacity and of in-ground reserves under contract to the pipelines. It concluded that rate levels would generate revenues to cover all prudent expenditures on service, including a compensatory return on capital outlays.

The commission's start-up effort, from the 1940s to the 1960s, centered on constraining transport prices for service and thus profits of pipeline companies. The three functions that the agency decided it had to manage to do so were: control of entry, control of profit returns, and control of specific prices. The process began with an application for a "certificate of public convenience and necessity" to introduce gas delivery into some set of wholesale markets. The application was examined for "sufficiency" of demand for the proposed service and capacity to provide the service. If certification was granted and service began, then proposals for price increases were submitted. If company and commission disagreed on the reasonableness of the proposed price schedule, a hearing examiner listened to opposing positions and offered a decision for consideration by the commission. If, in the view of the company, the commission's decision was not in accord with the statute or followed from the use of irregular procedures, then the applicant company appealed for a reversal in the federal courts.

Over the years the number of pipeline companies that came under FPC jurisdiction increased from a dozen to more than eighty. The combination of deciding certificate conditions and price schedule requirements made the commission's business an extensive activity. In 1970 more than eighty pipeline companies were under commission regulation with combined sales of $7.8 billion. In that year their combined operating costs were $5.6 billion, and for purposes of computing capital costs net plant was valued at $17.9 billion.[7]

The interstate pipelines in these early years had some of the characteristics of regional monopoly providers of a highly differentiated service with economies of scale in transmission and wide swings over the seasons in throughput. But with technical limits on pipe size, at approximately thirty-six inches in diameter, and demands growing to levels that allowed multiple companies, each with lines of that diameter, to serve a metropolitan region, entry and overlap of carriers grew widespread. More than three pipelines from different producing basins could take gas to the city gate to serve populations of more than two or three million.[8]

In its certification practices the commission set the terms and conditions of the wellhead purchase contracts of these pipelines. The interests of the regulator centered on security of delivery at the wellhead, from season to season and year to year. The contracts required that gas be provided over lengthy periods, from five to twenty years, making them inherently uncertain ventures. But certification from inception required the pipeline company to have field-purchase contracts with enough reserves to meet resale demands for throughput over the pipeline's lifetime. This requirement called for secured reserves but did not specify the price until delivery. That price, before direct wellhead price controls were applied in the 1960s, was frequently pegged to an "initial base price" on any newer contracts for comparable sales in the same field region.

In operation, a jurisdictional pipeline company had to justify increases in its tariff price schedule on the grounds that revenues to be generated from sales of gas and transportation at those prices were necessary to cover the costs of providing service. The commission's review centered on depreciation of prudent capital outlays and on "reasonable" rates of return to be allowed on the remaining book value of those outlays. Attempts were made to define a reasonable rate of return with precision. They led to detailed studies of comparable returns of other companies centered on the interest payments and dividends required to maintain the level of investment. In these proceedings financial experts provided assessments of comparable earnings and of capital market valuation of these earnings on investments of comparable risk. The process left it to the commission to sort out conflicting assessments and then announce the rate of return it would allow to be included in the costs of providing service.

The last of the three functions, regulatory analysis of particular prices, became quite specific. The commission devised, although it did not always apply, the so-called Atlantic Seaboard Formula, requiring half of capital costs to be allocated to customers on the basis of annual gas sales and half on the basis of sales during a designated peak demand period.[9] That allocation justified price differences on sales to buyers for baseload and for peak period consumption. Yet it failed because the pipelines could not make sales at the prices implied by the allocation of costs to off-peak periods. The commission applied the formula in some cases, but in other cases it ended up negotiating prices at lower levels that made sales possible.

The Federal Power Commission exercised review procedures to judge increases in more than 1,500 price schedules each year. Those requesting rate increases had their tariffs suspended, to be approved, rejected, or revised to meet commission requirements. On occasion, the commission initiated proceedings without waiting for a proposal in order to lower rate levels in a tariff.

Regulation of natural gas pipeline companies cost the Federal Power Commission about $3.5 million per year during the 1960s.[10] The costs for defendants and interveners could not have been much less. In 1968, for example, private costs of regulation incurred by the gas pipelines totaled $2.5 million.[11] The number of commission proceedings varied, increasing during periods of inflation, as requests for rate increases from pipelines all came in at the same time. If gas deliveries took place at lower prices because of regulation, then possibly the commission performed well. Almost any measure of benefits to consumers from lower prices would exceed these levels of costs. But as I shall show in Chapters 4 and 5, these benefits to consumers were not forthcoming.

WELLHEAD PRICE REGULATION

The 1954 Supreme Court *Phillips* decision required the commission to exercise jurisdiction over wellhead prices of natural gas producers on their sales to interstate pipelines. The first attempt replicated procedures for regulating pipeline sale prices, with "cost-based" limits on prices in each contract of every individual producer. The attempt failed because there were too many producers, too many contracts, and too many cost elements to determine regulated prices on each sale.

Faced with having to approve arbitrary price differences in cases that waited years for decisions, the commission turned to setting basin-wide price ceilings based on average costs of exploration and development. In 1960 it set provisional prices for "new" and "old" contracts in twenty-four producing regions and began proceedings to set permanent prices based on specific costs in each region. In 1968 the Supreme Court affirmed the legality of these "area rates" in approving ceilings for the Permian Basin in southwest Texas and New Mexico, the first basin for which the commission had completed the new procedure.[12]

This setting of area rates did not turn out to be a straightforward exercise. The proceedings were prolonged and required administrative resources far greater than expected. The Permian Basin case began in December 1960 with hearings on prices for contracts of 351 companies. The hearings, completed in September 1963, led to a commission decision in August 1965 and a Supreme Court decision in May 1968.[13] The commission subsequently put these ceilings into effect in 1968, in place of provisional prices announced in 1960, so that the first area price ceilings took almost eight years to be made effective.

The commission began six more proceedings in the late 1960s and early 1970s. Because the FPC could build upon the findings from the Permian Basin case, these later proceedings took less time, but the process was still both complex and tendentious. The lack of logic for determining relevant historical costs in order to set limits on future prices to expand future supply made it necessary to resort to judgments of a "reasonable" price. The commission fell back on data for later year average total costs across wells in a basin to define unreasonableness. But producers had not and did not undertake new well development projects at costs that exceeded the previously set provisional price limits. In effect, provisional prices determined permanent prices.

Area rate proceedings did not replace individual certificates of convenience and necessity for producers seeking to enter into contracts for newly discovered reserves and production. But individual reviews led to certification if reserves were to be produced at prices within provisional area-rate ceilings in that basin. Thus, producer certificate proceedings became the same as individual company area-rate proceedings, with new supplies going into wellhead markets at prices marked for old supplies.

The number of certificate proceedings was large. In the late 1960s, approximately two thousand applications for certificates were filed with the commission per year. About twelve hundred of these received attention within the year in which they were filed, and the remainder were attended to in the following year. This large number produced backlogs ranging up to nine months, and temporary certificates were issued so as not to delay production. In addition, applications for exceptions to provisional area ceilings were much more numerous. In 1969 the commission completed review of five hundred such applications for exceptions although more than seventy-five hundred had been filed;[14] in that year an additional eighty-four producer cases were completed that pertained to prices on gas from areas where provisional ceilings had not yet been set.

Area proceedings cost tens of millions of dollars each year. The commission at the end of the 1960s was spending more than $3 million annually on proceedings and decisions. The producers were undertaking detailed investigations of drilling and production costs to prepare findings for these proceedings. Total regulatory costs cannot be documented, but an indication of what these costs were is in the decision in the Permian Basin proceeding, which allowed producers 0.14 cents per thousand cubic feet (mcf) to recover expenses, and uncontested industry testimony in the Texas Gulf Coast area rate proceeding found that producer costs from regulation amounted to 0.15 cents per mcf in that proceeding.[15] Given that 75 percent of the 16 trillion cubic feet sold annually to the interstate pipelines was subject to one of these area rate proceedings, then 0.15 cents per mcf multiplied by that amount implies that producer costs incurred in the "streamlined" area rate proceedings were $18 million per annum in perpetuity.[16] The costs for the twelve hundred certificate applications and five hundred rate-increase applications processed must have taken the total costs to more than $20 million per annum. The cost of regulatory delay—that is, of the investment value of having to postpone production due to regulation—was likely greater than all of these dollar costs, but no estimate can be made of these expenses.[17]

Even doubling an estimate of $20 million, however, would not make the total costs of regulation large relative to potential consumer gains from regulation-imposed price reductions. The gas pipeline companies bought more than $4.5 billion of gas from producers in 1970.[18] If regulation did hold prices down by only 1 percent, then those buying at the lower price could have gained more than was spent in the regulatory process. Yet regulation did not have that result, so that no such benefits can be assessed against regulatory costs (see Chapter 3).

As a direct result of price ceilings at the wellhead, gas retail and wholesale markets experienced substantial shortages by the mid-1970s. These were manifest in curtailments of interruptible customers and refusals to connect new firm customers. Gas distributors were 10 percent short in 1974 and were as much as 20 percent short by 1977. Consumers in the Northeast and on the West Coast incurred a substantial shortage, but particularly those in the North Central region in the winter of 1976–1977 were short by as much as a half of what industrial and commercial establishments on gas systems were calling for. And yet buyers in the South were still able to obtain sufficient supply; by locating in a producing state, they were not in "interstate commerce" and thus were not subject to price controls. Where prices were controlled there was a shortage, but where prices were not controlled, there was plentiful supply.

Not only production but also consumer and producer welfare was disoriented by this regulation. Consumers taking from retail distributors for home service received billions of dollars in benefits in the ten years from 1968 to 1977 under the low ceiling prices. What they gained producers lost and more. Their losses, which would have gone at least in part into exploration and development, played a role in reducing the development of new field reserves beyond the end of the decade. The largest losers, however, were consumers who could not get on the delivery system or were partially curtailed; their losses were more than the gains of those consumers who received sufficient gas. Thus the price control process of the FPC benefited some consumers with low-priced gas by holding down their monthly bills, but inflicted greater losses on other consumers by causing them to go without low-priced gas. Buyers as a group, as well as producers as a group, lost by more than $20 billion over the ten-year period (see table 3.2).

The Federal Power Commission, given the task of regulating gas field prices by the Supreme Court, had failed in its implementation process. To make the United States less vulnerable to energy crises, the Carter administration sought to increase domestic energy supplies by formulating a new policy to eliminate gas shortages. The Natural Gas Policy Act of 1978 (NGPA) was enacted to provide the turn in regulatory direction that would restore supply-and-demand equilibrium, if not efficiency, to gas markets. Yet its goals went beyond clearing gas markets to preventing the producer of old contract reserves from benefiting from increases in gas prices. These contradictory goals—increase supply but hold down prices—were to be achieved by ending price controls on additional supply while retaining controls on already committed supply over substantial periods of time.

This elaborate price-discriminating process was applied not only to new and old interstate supplies but also to supplies shifted from intrastate into interstate markets, to deep and shallow supplies, and to offshore and onshore supplies. The act "defined" more than thirty classifications of gas, with only three involving production that would sell at unregulated prices immediately. These classes thus limited the amount of additional reserves available to expand production to interstate markets in the immediate period of shortage. And pipelines with large volumes of outstanding regulated (low-priced) reserves made high offer prices for new gas, because their low "weighted average cost of gas" could more easily be passed through to buyers. The new practice shifted supplies to New England and the West North Central region, given that the old gas price, the "cushion," was lowest for these northern pipelines.

By the early 1980s demand conditions in these markets did not any longer support the new gas contract prices. These prices had by then pushed up the average city-gate price, making gas at city gates too costly to be competitive with other industrial and commercial fuels. As a result, rates of take declined for the new gas under contract at the wellhead for resale to the gas distributors and industrial buyers. This difference between contract and actual take, the so-called bubble of excess supply, expanded to more one-quarter of potential throughput in the pipeline system in the next two years. Spot sales off-contract of the "bubble" were arranged at lower prices, and a new market was developed for unbundled, spot gas supplies at prices at least one dollar less per mcf than those for the contract gas of the pipelines.

As a result, the NGPA's effects on consumer and producer welfare differed from those of the price-ceiling regulation that preceded it. Prices in this regime were too high, rather than too low; even so, they had the same effect, that of reducing production below the level that would have been realized in unregulated wellhead markets. But now there developed two markets for production, the contract market and the new spot market. What producers gained consumers lost from the higher prices consumers in the contract, but what producers lost in having to dispose of surplus at low prices in the spot market was not made up by consumer gains in that market (see table 3.12). On the whole, participants in these markets were worse off as NGPA partial price decontrol worked through field and wholesale markets.

DEREGULATION

In 1985 the Federal Energy Regulatory Commission (FERC), the successor agency to the FPC, initiated a series of orders intended to restructure the buy-sell relationships among producing, transmission, and distribution companies. For more than fifty years, gas plus transportation had been provided in a "merchant" package by the interstate pipelines to retail distributors at the city gate. Gas production was from dedicated reserves under contract with field producers at the wellhead; if removal of impurities was required, or storage at the wellhead or at some intermediate transmission point, then these services were included in the bundle and charged for in the merchant service. FERC Order 436 made possible the unbundling of gas and transportation in 1985, allowing "open access" for consumers to ship their own gas and buy space in the pipelines. And thirty-five years after *Phillips,* Congress passed the Natural Gas Wellhead Decontrol Act of 1989, removing price controls on wellhead sales as of January 1993. Consumers, not only industrial but also commercial and institutional end users, were able to contract at the wellhead in an open, unregulated market with gas marketers or producers to bypass gas ownership by the pipeline company.

In new markets, for gas separate from transportation, independent source suppliers could provide gas for a day, a month, or a year, with that gas transported by any pipeline based on a contract for space. That restructuring of the industry was required universally in 1992 with FERC Order 636, which mandated that interstate pipelines offer transportation only. In effect, the pipelines had to remove themselves from the provision of merchant service, and instead provide space in their systems to producers, local distributing companies, or end-use consumers. The commission continued to regulate transportation prices, but now as charges for firm space. With the development of secondary markets for space previously committed, so that transportation could be obtained from sources (other shippers) besides the pipeline, the commission set new limits on secondary prices as well.

These changes have made gas markets since the mid-1990s structurally different from those in previous decades. Wellhead purchasers negotiate for spot, short-term, and long-term contract gas production at various rates of take. These brokers and dealers negotiate with transmission companies for transportation, based on being able to switch their gas from pipeline to pipeline through market hubs to destination.

The focal point of transactions has changed from contract reserves to spot current and future production. Higher prices bring forth more wellhead supplies and more pipeline firm transport capacity. Markets no longer operate on long-term contract obligation to provide service but, rather, on firm versus interruptible delivery of spot gas on a contract-by-contract basis. In pipeline operations, marketers with firm gas and transportation contracts specify monthly shipments, and other marketers with spot gas take interruptible transportation. Using electronic bulletin boards for offers and bids, for both gas and pipeline space, the marketer as agent for the consumer has access to current prices and to commodity exchange futures prices. Marketers and brokers operating in spot and futures prices bring about the convergence of production for deliveries to pipelines and distributors of sufficient gas to meet anticipated household and industrial demands.

SUMMARY

For forty years natural gas from various producing basins arrived at the city gate of a metropolitan region priced at levels controlled at the wellhead, again at the city gate, based on regulated rates for transportation services required for the delivery. After such regulatory practices produced first shortages and then excess supply, partial price deregulation was put in place, which gradually ended price controls at the wellhead as well as controls on some rates for transportation. In effect, gas was unbundled from transportation, at each level, by new regulatory actions. It is to be determined whether there were gains or losses to consumers, producers, or distributors at each stage.

Chapter 2 A Model of Natural
Gas Market Wellhead Prices
and Quantities

The characteristic feature of markets for gas that goes into pipelines is that wellhead prices in contracts for dedicated reserves bring total production in line with total demand for that production. Certain operating practices make this process converge to equilibrium with neither shortage nor excess supply over some period of time. Because production takes place under reserves contracts, supply needs to adjust to demands in a multiyear process. Excess demands in times of extreme cold weather are dealt with by increasing take from reserves but also by expanding take from storage and from "line pack" in the pipelines. Excess demands over longer periods are eliminated by a more complex process: higher prices in new contracts trigger price increases in existing contracts; these higher prices not only lead to additions to reserves and production but also curtail long-term demands.

ESTIMATION OF DEMAND
EQUATIONS

Consider first this characteristic set of relationships inherent in demands for natural gas. Production demand is marked by separate residential, industrial, commercial, and electric utility sectors. The substitution of gas for other energy products occurs at different rates in each sector. To account for these differences, the total demand for energy in each sector breaks down into gas and other fuel shares. Share equations for gas, petroleum, coal, and electricity differ in each sector. Total gas demand equals the sum of sectoral gas volumes over all four sectors.

The equation set constructed to estimate annual demand for natural gas production is seen in figure 2.1. The four sectoral energy-demand equations depend on "market size," as measured by industrial production or personal consumption expenditures, and on an index price that accounts for all four fuels. The share of total expenditures for each fuel in each sector is a function of its price, the prices for other fuels, and the previous period share. Because shares are percentages of expenditures, the share coefficient is positive if demand is inelastic and negative if demand is elastic.

Total gas demand across sectors is estimated in three stages. First, sectoral total energy demand is multiplied by the index of all-fuel prices to arrive at total sectoral expenditure. Second, sector expenditures are multiplied by gas share and divided by gas price to find sectoral gas demands.[1] Finally, total gas demands are the sum of the demands in these sectors.

DEMAND EQUATIONS

Total gas demand is shown in table 2.1 as "marketed production" for the period 1967 to 1995. The highest level of demand was realized in the early 1970s, at 22.6 trillion cubic feet in 1973. Demand fell to its lowest level, 16.9 trillion cubic feet, in 1983 and again in 1986. Production at peak was out of reserves of 224 trillion cubic feet, and at the lowest level it was out of reserves of 177 trillion cubic feet in 1983 and 165 trillion cubic feet in 1986. Rates-of-take from the contracted reserve base were roughly the same, at 1 cubic foot per 10 cubic feet of reserve, in this period.

Prices paid by consumers are shown in table 2.2. The industrial price in constant 1982 dollars doubled in the early 1970s, at the time when crude oil prices quadrupled in the so-called embargo. In market terms, gas prices paid by industry were matching those of alternative fuels as they were escalating. The residential price, also in constant 1982 dollars, increased only 25 percent in this same period and by only the same dollar amount as wellhead prices; both of these prices were regulated, whereas the industrial price was largely unregulated.

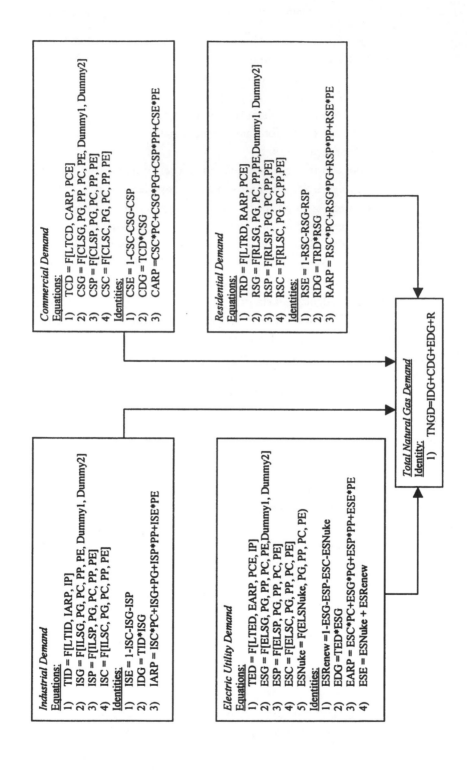

Commercial Demand
Equations:
1) TCD = F[LTCD, CARP, PCE]
2) CSG = F[CLSG, PG, PP, PC, PE, Dummy1, Dummy2]
3) CSP = F[CLSP, PG, PC, PP, PE]
4) CSC = F[CLSC, PG, PC, PP, PE]
Identities:
1) CSE = 1-CSC-CSG-CSP
2) CDG = TCD*CSG
3) CARP =CSC*PC+CSG*PG+CSP*PP+CSE*PE

Residential Demand
Equations:
1) TRD = F[LTRD, RARP, PCE]
2) RSG = F[RLSG, PG, PC, PP,PE,Dummy1, Dummy2]
3) RSP = F[RLSP, PG, PC,PP,PE]
4) RSC = F[RLSC, PG, PC,PP,PE]
Identities:
1) RSE = 1-RSC-RSG-RSP
2) RDG = TRD*RSG
3) RARP = RSC*PC+RSG*PG+RSP*PP+RSE*PE

Industrial Demand
Equations:
1) TID = F[LTID, IARP, IP]
2) ISG = F[ILSG, PG, PC, PP, PE, Dummy1, Dummy2]
3) ISP = F[ILSP, PG, PC, PP, PE]
4) ISC = F[ILSC, PG, PC, PP, PE]
Identities:
1) ISE = 1-ISC-ISG-ISP
2) IDG = TID*ISG
3) IARP = ISC*PC+ISG+PG+ISP*PP+ISE*PE

Electric Utility Demand
Equations:
1) TED = F[LTED, EARP, PCE, IP]
2) ESG = F[ELSG, PG, PP, PC, PE,Dummy1, Dummy2]
3) ESP = F[ELSP, PG, PP, PC, PE]
4) ESC = F[ELSC, PG, PP, PC, PE]
5) ESNuke = F(ELSNuke, PG, PP, PC, PE)
Identities:
1) ESRenew =1-ESG-ESP-ESC-ESNuke
2) EDG =TED*ESG
3) EARP = ESC*PC+ESG*PG+ESP*PP+ESE*PE
4) ESE = ESNuke + ESRenew

Total Natural Gas Demand
Identity:
1) TNGD=IDG+CDG+EDG+R

Figure 2.1. Flow diagram: natural gas demand

Variables are defined for the industrial sector. The definitions are the same for the other sectors; however, the values are specific to each sector.

TID: Total Industrial Demand

IARP: Estimator for Average Industrial Price of Gas

ISC: Coal's Share of Industrial Expenditure

ISE: Electricity's Share of Industrial Expenditure

ISP: Petroleum's Share of Industrial Expenditure

IDG: Industrial Demand for Gas

LTID: Lagged Total Industrial Demand

ILSC: Lagged Value Share of Coal (Ind.)

ILSG: Lagged Value Share of Gas (Ind.)

ILSP: Lagged Value Share of Petroleum (Ind.)

ILSE: Lagged Value Share of Electricity (Ind.)

TNGD: Total Demand for Natural Gas

PC: Real Price of Coal

PG: Real Price of Gas

PP: Real Price of Petroleum

PE: Real Price of Electricity

IP: Industrial Production

PCE: Personal Consumption Expenditures

Dummy1: Dummy variable for years 1968–1978

Dummy2: Dummy variable for years 1979–1984

Equations: 17   Identities: 14

21

Table 2.1. U.S. natural gas volumes

Year	Total new gas wells[1]	Marketed production	Net imports	Reserves[2,3]	Additions to reserves[4]	Cost per well[5,6] (dollars)
			Trillions of cubic feet			
1967	3,659	18.2	0.5	292.9	12.6	372,971.7
1968	3,456	19.3	0.6	287.3	7.1	375,900.5
1969	4,083	20.7	0.7	275.1	10.3	373,023.9
1970	4,031	21.9	0.8	264.7	10.0	368,052.5
1971	3,983	22.5	0.9	252.8	9.8	362,652.1
1972	5,484	22.5	0.9	240.1	6.4	330,127.1
1973	6,975	22.6	1.0	224.0	9.8	307,473.6
1974	7,170	21.6	0.9	211.1	12.7	344,449.6
1975	8,170	20.1	0.9	202.2	7.9	435,231.3
1976	9,438	20.0	0.9	190.0	12.8	424,961.6
1977	12,119	20.0	1.0	182.9	11.4	463,692.3
1978	14,405	20.0	0.9	174.3	14.6	514,312.7
1979	15,170	20.5	1.2	168.9	24.6	561,662.0
1980	17,223	20.2	0.9	173.0	22.9	622,546.0
1981	19,907	20.0	0.8	175.7	19.7	743,098.3
1982	18,944	18.6	0.9	175.5	17.3	864,278.0
1983	14,556	16.9	0.9	174.2	14.1	583,122.7
1984	17,012	18.3	0.8	171.5	14.2	452,378.7
1985	14,252	17.3	0.9	167.4	15.5	454,820.2
1986	8,135	16.9	0.7	165.6	12.5	454,785.5
1987	7,757	17.4	0.9	161.2	24.2	320,852.2
1988	8,238	17.9	1.2	168.0	17.0	374,758.2
1989	9,225	18.1	1.3	167.1	20.3	357,760.1
1990	10,705	18.6	1.4	169.3	16.3	352,957.2
1991	9,452	18.5	1.6	167.1	16.5	364,963.1
1992	8,091	18.7	1.9	165.0	16.1	298,705.9
1993	9,864	19.0	2.2	162.4	20.4	356,077.9
1994	8,977	19.7	2.5	163.8	21.0	357,602.9
1995	7,369	19.5	2.7	165.1	n/a	410,241.4

Source: DOE/EIA 1996, tables 4.5, 4.6, 4.10, 6.2, 6.3, app. D-1.

Notes: [1]Includes both exploration and development wells but not dry holes.

[2]EIA data beginning with 1980, which does not include gas in storage; AGA data for 1967–1979, which does include gas in storage.

[3]Beginning with 1965, all volumes are shown on a pressure base of 14.73 psia at 60°F; prior years use a pressure base of 14.65 psia at 60°F.

[4]Additions are computed from Reserves and Marketed Production data.

[5]In chained (1982) dollars, calculated using GDP implicit price deflators.

[6]Average cost is the arithmetic mean and includes all costs for drilling and equipping wells and for surface-producing facilities. Wells drilled include exploratory and development wells but exclude wells, stratigraphic tests, and core tests.

Table 2.2. Natural gas prices

Year	Nominal wellhead price[1] (c/mmBtu)	Real wellhead price[2] (c/mmBtu)	Nominal industrial price (c/mmBtu)	Real industrial price[3,4] (c/mmBtu)	Nominal residential price (c/mmBtu)	Real residential price[3] (c/mmBtu)
1967	15.5	41.0	32.9	87.15	100.8	266.58
1968	15.5	39.3	33.0	83.46	100.9	255.28
1969	16.5	39.9	33.9	82.06	101.8	246.18
1970	16.5	37.8	35.9	82.21	105.7	242.19
1971	17.5	38.0	39.8	86.57	111.5	242.83
1972	18.5	38.7	43.8	91.69	117.8	246.54
1973	21.5	42.7	49.0	97.07	126.5	250.44
1974	29.3	53.3	65.4	119.13	139.6	254.27
1975	43.1	71.6	94.1	156.34	167.6	278.48
1976	56.9	89.4	121.7	191.26	194.3	305.40
1977	77.4	114.4	147.2	217.70	230.6	341.06
1978	89.3	122.7	167.3	229.99	252.0	346.33
1979	115.6	146.5	195.5	247.80	292.7	371.07
1980	155.0	179.9	250.0	290.15	359.4	417.09
1981	192.8	205.1	306.3	325.87	418.5	445.21
1982	239.3	239.3	377.2	377.20	503.9	503.90
1983	251.2	240.9	405.4	388.79	587.8	563.66
1984	258.0	238.3	409.7	378.40	594.2	548.77
1985	243.2	217.5	383.1	342.56	593.6	530.76
1986	188.3	163.8	313.9	273.00	566.6	492.76
1987	162.0	136.6	285.2	240.55	537.3	453.28
1988	164.2	133.7	286.7	233.41	531.6	432.80
1989	163.9	128.1	287.1	224.37	547.0	427.51
1990	165.9	124.2	284.5	213.05	563.1	421.73
1991	159.2	114.7	260.9	187.97	564.5	406.70
1992	168.9	118.4	275.5	193.10	571.3	400.47
1993	198.6	135.7	298.6	204.04	599.2	409.41
1994	180.0	120.3	296.4	198.07	622.9	416.28
1995	150.9	98.3	263.9	171.91	590.1	384.42
1996	219.1	140.0	325.2	207.82	613.4	392.00

Source: DOE/EIA, 1996, tables 6.8, 6.9, apps. A-4, D-1.

Notes: [1]Converted from c/mcf to c/mmBtu using dry production heat content.

[2]In chained (1982) cents, calculated using GDP implicit price deflators.

[3]Converted from c/mcf to c/mmBtu using nonutility consumption heat content.

[4]Represents price of gas sold and delivered by local distribution companies and does not reflect gas transported for the others.

As the gas take rate of consumers declined in the early 1980s, however, industrial and residential prices decreased. The constant dollar industrial price peaked in 1983 at $3.88 per mcf to fall to $2.73 per mcf in 1986, while the constant dollar residential price was $5.63 mcf in 1983 and $4.92 per mcf in 1986. The demands for gas in industry and home consumption were decreasing.

These data for quantities and prices make up a set of annual observations for the period 1960–1995. Observations for each year for the determining variables were compiled so that thirty-six annual observations formed a data set for estimating demand equations.[2]

The share equations are shown in tables 2.3 through 2.6. They belong to a class of simultaneous equations fitted by Two-Stage Least Squares procedures. In the first stage, values for the endogenous variables on the right-hand side of the equations were estimated from ordinary least squares regressions of these variables on all exogenous variables. Those endogenous variables are the price of gas (PG) and four sectoral average energy prices (IARP, CARP, RARP, and EARP). In the second stage, ordinary least squares regressions of the endogenous dependent variables are estimated on the exogenous and fitted endogenous variables from the first stage.

These equations trace the historical data closely, as indicated by R-square estimates in the range from 0.735 to 0.995.[3] Total sectoral demands are determined by the energy price index and by either industrial or personal consumption (that is, these independent variables have statistically significant coefficients). Gas shares are elastic in industrial and residential markets, and inelastic in commercial markets, but only the industrial price is statistically significant. The gas share equations explain a substantial percentage of variation in year-to-year gas share of total demand, given that the R-square estimates range from 0.735 in residential share to 0.912 for commercial share.

Event period variables are included to account for the regulatory impact on demand. Binary (0,1) variables for the "price cap" years 1968–1978, and the "phased deregulation" years 1979–1984, have been included in the determinants of gas share in each sector. For the price cap years, residential and commercial gas shares were lower and industrial share was higher. For the phased deregulation years, residential and commercial gas shares were higher, while industrial share was lower. In all periods, lagged demand variables were current period-demand determinants as indicated by large and significant coefficients for these lagged variables.

Table 2.3. Industrial demand for natural gas

Regression equations		Total demand equation	Share equation no. 1	Share equation no. 2	Share equation no. 3
Dependent variable		TID	ISG	ISP	ISC
Description		Total Industrial Energy Demand	Industrial Share Gas	Industrial Share Petroleum	Industrial Share Coal

Independent variable

Name	Description				
Intercept	n/a	4.954 (3.66)	0.185 (3.56)	0.141 (3.11)	−0.027 (−1.82)
LTID	Lagged Total Industrial Demand	0.791 (12.27)	n/a	n/a	n/a
ILSG	Lagged Industrial Share Gas	n/a	0.720 (11.40)	n/a	n/a
ILSP	Lagged Industrial Share Petroleum	n/a	n/a	0.806 (10.00)	n/a
ILSC	Lagged Industrial Share Coal	n/a	n/a	n/a	0.940 (19.56)
IARP	Average Industrial Energy Price	−0.536 (−4.51)	n/a	n/a	n/a
IP	Industrial Production	0.027 (3.19)	n/a	n/a	n/a
PG	Price of Gas	n/a	−0.018 (−3.13)	0.028 (4.21)	−0.004 (−0.49)
PG	Price of Coal	n/a	−0.034 (−4.97)	0.028 (6.03)	0.001 (0.25)
PP	Price of Petroleum	n/a	0.011 (4.90)	−0.009 (−4.76)	−3.809e-04 (−0.17)
PE	Price of Electricity	n/a	−0.002 (−0.93)	−0.003 (−2.12)	0.003 (1.59)
Dummy1	Dummy variable for years 1968–1978	n/a	0.009 (1.74)	n/a	n/a
Dummy2	Dummy variable for years 1979–1984	n/a	−0.004 (−0.92)	n/a	n/a
	Durbin H-statistic	−0.347	−2.192**	−2.601**	−0.967
	Adjusted R-squared	0.869	0.959	0.957	0.979

Source: Data for 1960–1995 from *The Basic Petroleum Handbook* (American Petroleum Institute), *Monthly Energy Review* (DOE/EIA), and *Natural Gas Annual* (DOE/EIA).

Notes: The *t*-statistics are shown in parentheses below the coefficients.

*Indicates Durbin H-statistic is undefined, M-statistic shown instead.

**Indicates that two-step estimator was used (see Hatanaka 1974).

Table 2.4. Commercial demand for natural gas

Regression equations		Total demand equation	Share equation no. 1	Share equation no. 2	Share equation no. 3
Dependent variable		TCD	CSG	CSP	CSC
Description		Total Commercial Energy Demand	Commercial Share Gas	Commercial Share Petroleum	Commercial Share Coal
Independent variable					
Name	Description				
Intercept	n/a	0.558 (3.44)	0.366 (2.88)	−0.006 (−0.28)	−0.013 (−1.14)
LTCD	Lagged Total Commercial Demand	0.860 (14.27)	n/a	n/a	n/a
CLSG	Lagged Commercial Share Gas	n/a	0.516 (2.86)	n/a	n/a
CLSP	Lagged Commercial Share Petroleum	n/a	n/a	0.992 (22.35)	n/a
CLSC	Lagged Commercial Share Coal	n/a	n/a	n/a	0.859 (24.09)
CARP	Estimator for Average Commercial Energy Price	−0.040 (−1.97)	n/a	n/a	n/a
PCE	Personal Consumption Expenditures	2.628e-04 (2.32)	n/a	n/a	n/a
PG	Price of Gas	n/a	0.014 (0.87)	0.017 (1.33)	−0.002 (−0.38)
PP	Price of Petroleum	n/a	0.004 (0.82)	−0.008 (−2.29)	7.112e-05 (0.07)
PG	Price of Coal	n/a	0.029 (1.81)	0.008 (1.06)	−3.311e-04 (−0.11)
PE	Price of Electricity	n/a	−0.016 (−2.59)	0.001 (0.44)	0.001 (0.95)
Dummy1	Dummy variable for years 1968–1978	n/a	−0.008 (−0.77)	n/a	n/a
Dummy2	Dummy variable for years 1979–1984	n/a	0.004 (0.38)	n/a	n/a
	Durbin H-statistic	0.057	−0.788*	−1.218	−1.422
	Adjusted R-squared	0.978	0.905	0.980	0.993

Source: Data for 1960–1995 from *The Basic Petroleum Handbook* (American Petroleum Institute), *Monthly Energy Review* (DOE/EIA), and *Natural Gas Annual* (DOE/EIA).

Notes: The t-statistics are shown in parentheses below the coefficients.

*Indicates Durbin H-statistic is undefined, M-statistic shown instead.

Table 2.5. Residential demand for natural gas

Regression equations		Total demand equation	Share equation no. 1	Share equation no. 2	Share equation no. 3
Dependent variable		TRD	RSG	RSP	RSC
Description		Total Residential Demand	Residential Share Gas	Residential Share Petroleum	Residential Share Coal
Independent variable					
Name	Description				
Intercept	n/a	1.503	0.250	0.015	−0.004
		(4.19)	(3.89)	(0.80)	(−1.11)
LTRD	Lagged Total Residential Demand	0.814	n/a	n/a	n/a
		(16.13)			
RLSG	Lagged Residential Share Gas	n/a	0.601	n/a	n/a
			(5.23)		
RLSP	Lagged Residential Share Petroleum	n/a	n/a	0.957	n/a
				(20.03)	
RLSC	Lagged Residential Share Coal	n/a	n/a	n/a	0.852
					(38.57)
RARP	Average Residential Price	−0.138	n/a	n/a	n/a
		(−4.19)			
PCE	Personal Consumption Expenditures	4.662e-04	n/a	n/a	n/a
		(3.77)			
PG	Price of Gas	n/a	−0.007	0.017	−0.001
			(−1.05)	(1.57)	(−0.61)
PP	Price of Petroleum	n/a	2.025e-04	−0.010	1.999e-04
			(0.08)	(−3.60)	(0.86)
PG	Price of Coal	n/a	0.012	0.004	−2.209e-04
			(1.35)	(0.56)	(−0.37)
PE	Price of Electricity	n/a	−0.003	0.001	2.523e-04
			(−1.80)	(0.71)	(0.94)
Dummy1	Dummy variable for years 1968–1978	n/a	−0.013	n/a	n/a
			(−2.11)		
Dummy2	Dummy variable for years 1979–1984	n/a	0.019	n/a	n/a
			(3.29)		
	Durbin H-statistic	0.195	−1.566	−0.188	−2.102*
	Adjusted R-squared	0.952	0.735	0.985	0.996

Source: Data for 1960–1995 from *The Basic Petroleum Handbook* (American Petroleum Institute), *Monthly Energy Review* (DOE/EIA), and *Natural Gas Annual* (DOE/EIA).

Notes: The *t*-statistics are shown in parentheses below the coefficients.

*Indicates that two-step estimator was used (see Hatanaka 1974).

Table 2.6. Electric utility demand for natural gas

Regression equations		Total demand equation	Share equation no. 1	Share equation no. 2	Share equation no. 3	Share equation no. 4
Dependent variable		TED	ESG	ESP	ESC	ESNuke
Description		Total Electric Demand	Electric Share Gas	Electric Share Petroleum	Electric Share Coal	Electric Share Nuclear
Independent variable						
Name	Description					
Intercept	n/a	0.795 (1.42)	0.005 (0.14)	0.072 (2.83)	0.032 (0.60)	0.017 (0.86)
LTED	Lagged Total Electric Utility Demand for Gas	0.905 (13.31)	n/a	n/a	n/a	n/a
ELSG	Lagged Electric Utility Share Gas	n/a	0.885 (12.41)	n/a	n/a	n/a
ELSP	Lagged Electric Utility Share Petroleum	n/a	n/a	1.018 (10.45)	n/a	n/a
ELSC	Lagged Electric Utility Share Coal	n/a	n/a	n/a	0.773 (6.37)	n/a
ELSNuke	Lagged Electric Utility Share Nuclear	n/a	n/a	n/a	n/a	1.014 (33.44)
EARP	Average Residential Price	−0.091 (−0.79)	n/a	n/a	n/a	n/a
PCE	Personal Consumption Expenditures	−0.001 (−1.13)	n/a	n/a	n/a	n/a
IP	Industrial Production	0.060 (1.91)	n/a	n/a	n/a	n/a
PG	Estimator for Price of Gas	n/a	−0.022 (−1.75)	0.024 (3.17)	−0.004 (−0.39)	0.010 (1.04)
PP	Price of Petroleum	n/a	0.002 (0.49)	−0.011 (−4.14)	0.004 (0.98)	−0.004 (−1.31)
PG	Price of Coal	n/a	−0.013 (−0.95)	−0.001 (−0.04)	−0.024 (−1.32)	0.013 (2.09)
PE	Price of Electricity	n/a	0.002 (0.72)	−0.003 (−1.33)	0.006 (2.18)	−0.001 (−0.78)
Dummy1	Dummy variable for years 1968–1978	n/a	2.672e-05 (0.003)	n/a	n/a	n/a
Dummy2	Dummy variable for years 1979–1984	n/a	0.015 (1.40)	n/a	n/a	n/a
	Durbin H-statistic	1.472	1.319	0.343	0.455	0.306
	Adjusted R-squared	0.996	0.967	0.971	0.929	0.988

Source: Data for 1960–1995 from *The Basic Petroleum Handbook* (American Petroleum Institute), *Monthly Energy Review* (DOE/EIA), and *Natural Gas Annual* (DOE/EIA).

Notes: The *t*-statistics are shown in parentheses below the coefficients.

*Indicates Durbin H-statistic is undefined, M-statistic shown instead.

ESTIMATION OF SUPPLY EQUATIONS

The supply side of the model consists of six equations. The first equation is for gas well drilling, which depends on previous period well drilling, gas and crude oil prices, and the relevant regulatory regime. This drilling activity then generates reserve discoveries and leads to revisions and extensions of old reserves.

The two equations for discoveries are for determinants of the number of new discovery wells and of the mean size of new reserves per discovery well. New discovery wells are a function of previous period discovery wells, gas and oil prices, and the presence or absence of a regulatory regime. The average new volume of reserves per new discovery well is a function of previous period gas price, total new wells, and the regulatory regime.

The two equations for revision and extension of reserves take the same structure; the first determines the number of development wells, and the second determines the revision and extension of gas reserves per new development well. The number of development wells depends on new exploratory wells, previous period wells, the gas price, and the size of previous revisions and extensions. The regulatory regime in place at the time plays a role. Variables have been included for regulation on the hypothesis that the regulatory regime changes development activity all else being equal.

Together, discoveries and revisions or extensions determine additions to reserves. The rate-of-take from reserves determines the amount of production, with this rate as a function of wells, industrial production, and lagged rate-of-take. The sequence in which these relationships generate supply is shown in figure 2.2.

The equations for supply fitted to the price and quantity data are shown in table 2.7. The first equation for total gas wells indicates that increases in the number of wells have been associated with gas and oil price increases (although the coefficients of the price variables are not statistically significant). Previous period well installation rates have been positive and significant in year-to-year levels of total wells.

Once the number of wells is determined, the equation set separates activity between wildcat wells to locate new reserves and development wells to add further to old reserves. Wildcat wells have been determined by three variables, changes in oil and gas prices and lagged wildcat wells, all of which have positive and significant coefficients. The development well completion rate has been determined by the gas price, which has a positive and significant coefficient, and the change in total wells, with a positive and significant coefficient. The

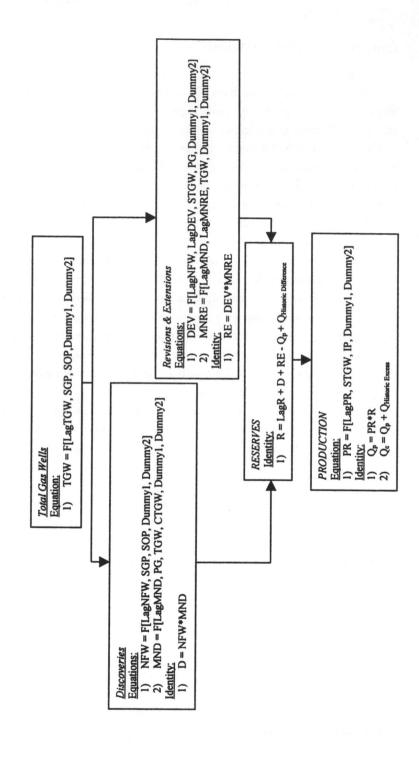

Total Gas Wells
Equation:
1) TGW = F[LagTGW, SGP, SOP,Dummy1, Dummy2]

Discoveries
Equations:
1) NFW = F[LagNFW, SGP, SOP, Dummy1, Dummy2]
2) MND = F[LagMND, PG, TGW, CTGW, Dummy1, Dummy2]
Identity:
1) D = NFW*MND

Revisions & Extensions
Equations:
1) DEV = F[LagNFW, LagDEV, STGW, PG, Dummy1, Dummy2]
2) MNRE = F[LagMND, LagMNRE, TGW, Dummy1, Dummy2]
Identity:
1) RE = DEV*MNRE

RESERVES
Identity:
1) R = LagR + D + RE - Q_p + $Q_{Historic\ Difference}$

PRODUCTION
Equation:
1) PR = F[LagPR, STGW, IP, Dummy1, Dummy2]
Identity:
1) Q_p = PR*R
2) Q_c = Q_p + $Q_{Historic\ Excess}$

Figure 2.2. Flow diagram: natural gas supply

TGW: Total Gas Wells
STGW: % Change in TGW
CTGW: Cumulative TGW
LagTGW: Lagged Value of Total Gas Wells
SGP: % Change in Gas Price
SOP: % Change in Oil Price
NFW: New Field Wildcats
LagNFW: Lagged Value of New Field Wildcats
MND: New Discoveries per New Field Wildcat
LagMND: Lagged Value of Mean New Discoveries per New Field Wildcat
D: New Discoveries
DEV: Development Wells
LagDEV: Lagged Value of Developmental Wells

MNRE: Revisions & Extensions over Development Wells
RE: Revisions & Extensions
PR: Production-Reserve Ratio
LagPR: Lagged Value of Production-Reserve Ratio
Q_p: Production
Q_c: Consumption
IP: Industrial Production
R: Reserves
LagR: Lagged Value of Reserves
$Q_{Historic\ Excess}$: Historic Excess Demand
$Q_{Historic\ Difference}$: Historic balancing item
Dummy1: Dummy variable for years 1968–1978
Dummy2: Dummy variable for years 1979–1984

Equations: 6   Identities: 5

Table 2.7. Natural gas supply

Regression equations

| Dependent variable | TGW | NFW | MND | DEV | MNRE | PR |
| Description | Total Gas Wells | New Field Wells | Mean New Discoveries | Development Wells | Mean New Revisions and Extensions | Production-Reserve Ratio |

| Independent variable | | | | | | | |
Name	Description						
Intercept	n/a	1066.380 (1.31)	147.691 (1.73)	0.000	463.629 (0.83)	0.000	0.005 (2.83)
SGP	Change in Gas Price	5564.133 (1.69)	754.476 (1.94)	n/a	n/a	n/a	n/a
PG	Gas Price	n/a	n/a	−0.001 (−0.47)	2346.686 (2.21)	n/a	n/a
SOP	Change in Oil Prices	2989.180 (1.10)	476.555 (1.57)	n/a	n/a	n/a	n/a
IP	Industrial Production	n/a	n/a	n/a	n/a	n/a	2.991e-04 (5.06)
TGW	Total Gas Wells	n/a	n/a	−1.27e-07 (0.60)	n/a	3.716e-08 (1.63)	n/a
LagTGW	Lagged Total Gas Wells	0.832 (9.20)	n/a	n/a	n/a	n/a	n/a
STGW	Change in Total Gas Wells	n/a	n/a	n/a	10070.622 (5.62)	n/a	0.019 (5.12)

		(1)	(2)	(3)	(4)	(5)	(6)
CTGW	Cumulative Gas Wells	n/a	n/a	5.372e-09 (0.60)	n/a	n/a	n/a
LagNFW	Lagged New Field Wells	n/a	0.762 (7.86)	n/a	1.250 (1.45)	n/a	n/a
LagDev	Lagged Developmental Wells	n/a	n/a	n/a	0.456 (2.28)	n/a	n/a
LagMND	Lagged Mean New Discoveries	n/a	n/a	0.863 (8.56)	n/a	0.110 (2.23)	n/a
LagMNRE	Lagged Mean New Revisions and Extensions	n/a	n/a	n/a	n/a	0.625 (4.61)	n/a
LagPR	Lagged Production/Reserve Ratio	n/a	n/a	n/a	n/a	n/a	0.668 (10.63)
Dummy1	Dummy variable for years 1968–1978	190.783 (0.26)	69.817 (0.87)	−0.001 (−0.90)	−409.111 (−0.73)	−0.001 (−3.35)	0.003 (2.47)
Dummy2	Dummy variable for years 1979–1984	1235.313 (1.05)	169.486 (1.15)	−1.221e-03 (−0.66)	227.338 (0.24)	−0.001 (−1.79)	0.003 (1.57)
	Durbin H-statistic	−0.634	−0.482	−0.412	−1.743*	−1.235	−0.026
	Adjusted R-squared	0.897	0.915	0.561	0.939	0.758	0.988

Source: Data for 1960–1995 from *The Basic Petroleum Handbook* (American Petroleum Institute), *Monthly Energy Review* (DOE/EIA), and *Natural Gas Annual* (DOE/EIA).

Notes: The *t*-statistics are shown in parentheses below the coefficients.

*Indicates Durbin *H*-statistic is undefined, *M*-statistic shown instead.

**Indicates that two-step estimator was used (see Hatanaka 1974).

one-period lagged rate of completion of wildcat wells has a positive but insignificant effect on the number of new development wells. That the accumulation of new reserves has been a two-stage process of discovery and development is borne out by these fitted equations.

As the process of adding reserves takes place, both the amount found in new discoveries declines and the amount added in extensions of old reserves declines. In effect, diminishing returns for location set in. The size of a new discovery decreases (that is, the coefficient of the total wells variable in the mean new discovery equation is negative) and the coefficient for the lagged size of discoveries is less than one. The size of an average extension or revision of old reserves, however, increases with total wells so that only the low estimated value of the coefficient for lagged extensions or revisions (0.625 and significant) brings about diminishing returns. As the size of new discoveries has declined, then extensions and revisions have or have not declined, depending on price and total wells, relative to the lagged value.

Additions to reserves in a given year have been the product of number of wells times additions per well. That is, newly discovered reserves equal new field wildcat wells times new discoveries per well, and old reserve revisions or extensions equal new development wells times revisions added per new well. The sum of these two equals new reserves to provide the capacity for additional production. Gas supply equals the rate of production out of these reserves.

The production rate-of-take is scheduled to meet demands but is limited by the capacity for production (by total wells and the previous rate-of-take). The equation, as shown in table 2.7, has significant coefficients for industrial production, the change in total wells, and the lagged rate-of-take (with an R-square of 0.98). Production in a given year equals current reserves multiplied by this rate of production from reserves.

The regulatory regime has played a role as a determinant of supply. The coefficient for the binary variable for the 1968–1978 period of price caps shows that the production-reserve ratio was increased, but revisions or extensions were reduced. The binary variable for the second regulatory period had a negative but not significant coefficient for mean new extensions or revisions. In the first period, with price limits in place, the regime reduced reserves and increased the rate-of-take, whereas in the second period the new regulatory regime reduced reserves only marginally.

The supply and demand equations together describe the operations of markets at the consumer purchase level of demand and the wellhead level of supply. Market behavior is affected by regulatory activity that centers on the late 1960s to middle 1970s, when wellhead price caps were put in place by the Federal Power Commission, and on the period from the late 1970s to mid-1980s, when the Federal Energy Regulatory Commission implemented phased price decontrol under the Natural Gas Policy Act of 1978.

The responses of industry to regulation of one type or another determined market performance. The supply and demand system can be solved for production equal to demand, but while setting the regulatory variables at zero so as to specify "market-determined" price. This price would have been realized in the absence of price caps in the first period and phased decontrol in the second period. The difference between this price and historical price is the measure of how much market price was distorted by regulation. Note that this measurement process is adopted instead of estimating supply-and-demand equations for each regulatory period and observing how they changed; separate equations sets cannot be fitted with annual observations of production and price given that sample size for a regulatory period is only from six to eleven observations each.

SUMMARY

The wide swing in gas prices from 1983 peak to 1995 trough can be replicated by equations that account for the policies of regulatory agencies and associated responses of producers in field markets and consumers in wholesale or retail markets. A model construct in which supply of production out of reserves interacts with demands for gas as energy fuel and industrial raw material is developed here to describe these relationships. The extent to which the model reproduces actual behavior is indicated in table 2.8. Historical levels of consumption ("demand") and of production ("supply") are shown in columns 1 and 3, respectively.[4] The model generates estimates for demand, and separately for supply, by inserting actual values of determining variables in the appropriate equations for each year. That is, the model estimates of demand, in column 2, and of supply, in column 4, follow from inserting price, actual reserves, prices of other fuels, and other exogenous variables into relevant equations.

These model estimates over the thirty-year period simulate actual behavior closely but with some exception. Model supply on average over the period equals 18.48 trillion cubic feet per year, whereas actual supply was 18.64 trillion cubic feet, so that the model simulation is close. Model demand equals 19.28 trillion cubic feet, whereas actual demands were 18.03 trillion cubic feet, so that model demand is an overestimate of actual values. For the price cap period, the

Table 2.8. Fit of the supply-demand model with regulation (tcf)

Year	Demand		Supply	
	Actual	*Simulated*	*Actual*	*Simulated*
1962	13.33	14.74	13.72	14.07
1963	13.98	15.47	14.51	14.66
1964	14.85	16.25	15.30	15.07
1965	15.26	17.15	15.78	16.94
1966	16.45	17.75	17.01	17.36
1967	17.37	18.88	17.94	18.36
1968	18.60	19.89	19.07	20.76
1969	20.01	21.09	20.45	21.72
1970	20.95	22.11	21.52	20.93
1971	21.60	22.92	22.12	21.94
1972	21.90	23.51	22.06	22.34
1973	21.85	23.95	22.05	22.40
1974	21.05	23.34	21.06	22.27
1975	19.38	21.90	19.48	20.40
1976	19.82	20.47	19.25	19.20
1977	19.43	20.81	19.37	18.74
1978	19.53	20.57	19.27	18.41
1979	20.07	21.27	19.84	19.41
1980	19.73	21.56	19.69	18.96
1981	19.27	21.07	19.46	18.93
1982	17.90	19.91	18.05	18.91
1983	16.84	18.63	16.31	17.52
1984	17.96	18.07	17.67	17.08
1985	17.32	18.78	16.66	16.88
1986	16.22	18.70	16.21	15.84
1987	17.21	18.25	16.78	16.10
1988	17.93	19.37	17.19	16.67
1989	18.74	20.24	17.43	17.88
1990	18.60	21.17	18.01	17.73
1991	18.98	21.42	17.87	17.92
1992	19.53	21.66	17.95	17.75
1993	20.20	22.01	18.18	18.37
1994	20.65	22.83	18.91	17.99

Source: As explained in the text.

model exceeds historical demands by 1.49 trillion cubic feet per annum. For the phased deregulation period, model demands were again on average 1.40 trillion cubic feet too high. Market model values for supply replicate historic supply, but model values for demand exceed actual demands by 8 percent. In periods of intense regulatory activity, demands were less than model or "expected" demands, principally in industrial markets. Chapter 3 provides a detailed analysis of these extraordinary effects of regulation on these supplies and demands.

Chapter 3 The Regulation of Gas Field Contracts and the Resulting Gains and Losses from Market Performance

In the 1960s, the Federal Power Commission put in place a system of price controls on field gas purchase contracts. Having been required by the Supreme Court to set limits on these prices, the commission sought to make the new regulatory system operate so as to result in "reasonable" wellhead prices to industry and households throughout the country. "Reasonable" prices were to be defined as those in line with costs of gas reserve discovery and development and ultimately costs of production of gas to be injected into the pipeline transmission network.

To accomplish this goal, the commission in the 1960s required pipelines to contract for volumes of reserves sufficient to meet consumers' demands for the 1970s. Production from reserves was to be sufficient to fill the pipelines on peak demand days to provide service at the city gate for gas plus transport "merchant" service, available to industry and local distributing companies on demand.

The Supreme Court decision in *Phillips Petroleum v. Wisconsin* in 1954 had set direct controls over prices in wellhead contracts.[1] For more than a decade thereafter, various methods of control were tried that extended rate-setting practices to new limits. These methods failed; although they initially did constrain prices on field supplies of gas, they did not achieve the goal of contracting for reserves sufficient to meet demands.

This chapter chronicles the emergence of this regulatory regime and the performance of gas field markets that resulted. When price-cap regulation failed, it was replaced with a complex system of selective decontrol of prices on just supplies from certain production horizons. This partial deregulation, in turn, was intended to improve market performance—that is, to develop more gas reserves and production for consumers. The results again turned out to belie the intentions: consumers and producers lost from prices too high and from production also too high.

THE FOUNDATIONS OF FEDERAL REGULATION

Gas regulation has been built on existing practices of regulatory agencies in other industries, and "the history of a regulatory program may be as important as its governing statute and required rules of procedure in understanding particular policies."[2] Certain aspects of the history of regulation explain why procedures put in place to control gas prices took the form they did.

The first agency created by Congress to control an industry's pricing was the Interstate Commerce Commission (ICC), which under the Act to Regulate Commerce (1887) was to regulate railroad rates on service between the grain-, cattle-, and oil-producing regions in the West and the manufacturing centers in the East. The ICC was established as a result of initiatives of several interest groups, including such railway systems as the Baltimore and Ohio, the Pennsylvania, and the New York Central in the Mid-Atlantic and Great Lakes Regions. They and others had expanded with growth in the size of markets and in commodity exchanges at major rail hubs. By 1880 these railroads transported three times the volume of a decade earlier of agricultural and manufacturing commodities between such trading centers as Chicago and St. Louis in the Midwest and New York, Philadelphia, Boston, and Baltimore in the East. Because the cities were served by two or three and in some cases as many as five railroads, the rates ranged between cartel (monopoly) and competitive levels. The determinant was most likely whether the conditions were present for sustaining the cartel price schedule or whether, to the contrary, suppliers could profit from each lowering that price schedule. In fact, price wars were frequent, and numerous attempts to establish stable cartel rates failed, so that actual rates varied from three times cost to levels barely covering costs.[3]

This situation continued until Congress passed the Act to Regulate Commerce to authorize federal control of railroad rates on interstate merchandise and commodity shipments. Those who benefited included shippers in the East served by only one or two railroads; they had been charged higher rates for short hauls, for example, between Harrisburg, Pennsylvania, and New York City, than for long hauls by five or six railroads between major hubs, such as Chicago (via Harrisburg and other routes) and New York City. A second affected group included farmers east of Chicago who paid more for sending grain to New York City than did farmers in Iowa.

The Act to Regulate Commerce made it illegal to charge higher prices for shorter than for longer-distance services over the same line. It also required the railroads to file rates with the Interstate Commerce Commission, and empowered the ICC to enforce filed rates.[4] The resulting rates were stable at cartel-set levels in the first eight years after the establishment of the ICC; thereafter, as the courts challenged the commission's power and the jurisdiction of commission controls lagged behind the scope of the surface transportation market, rail rates once again varied from month to month over a range from cartel to competitive levels. Regardless of this outcome, the regulatory attempt to set stable rates to prevent discounting established the pattern of cartel rates.[5]

In its 1898 decision in *Smyth v. Ames,* the Supreme Court established the conceptual basis for all rates set by regulatory agencies. Given that a company had a right to profitable use of its property, the Court established that the company had to have an opportunity to recover the fair value of its investments in plant and equipment from regulated prices and quantities. Prices were to be determined on "the original cost of construction, the amount expended in permanent improvements, the amount and market value of its bonds and stocks, the present and original cost of plant and equipment, the earning capacity of the property under particular rates prescribed the stature, and the amount required to meet operating expenses." The Court did not specify which of these standards should be employed but, rather, stated that standards were required to set regulatory limits on prices.[6]

In the several decades of interpreting *Smyth v. Ames,* the courts and agencies have established procedures for determining prices based on concepts of comparable or "fair" returns on investment. Although at early stages they were involved in adjudicating minute details, to the point of declaring that rates approved by the agencies were too low or too high by a certain amount, eventually the courts realized that they lacked the expertise to decide exact prices case by case. The Supreme Court promulgated the "end result" test in 1944 in *FPC v.*

Hope Natural Gas Co., stating that "it is the result reached not the method employed, which is controlling. . . . It is not theory but the impact of the rate order which counts. If the total effect of the rate order cannot be said to be unjust and unreasonable, judicial inquiry under the [Natural Gas] Act is at an end." In this case, the Court also held that the agency is "not bound to the use of any single formula or combination of formulae in determining rates." Therefore, an agency would only have to assert to a challenger that "would upset the rate order" that it is "just and reasonable in its consequences."[7]

Regulatory practice was put in place for natural gas in the Natural Gas Act of 1938 (NGA). The Federal Power Commission was given the mandate to regulate interstate sales for resale of gas purchased by pipelines from producers. By 1955 the commission had a stated position for how this was to be done: "The Commission, in administering the rate regulation provisions of the Gas Act, has the primary obligation of prescribing rates that are just and reasonable to protect the interests of utility customers, while at the same time safeguarding the rights of investors to the end that new capital will be attracted to permit companies to carry out their functions in a manner conducive to orderly expansion necessary to meet consumer needs."[8] In 1954, the Supreme Court in *Phillips Petroleum Co. v. Wisconsin* ruled that under the NGA the commission had jurisdiction over the first sale in the field to the interstate pipeline and should exercise that authority by setting prices for production in the field contracts.[9] In this way the industry became regulated on all transactions from wellhead to pipeline resale at the city gate. The only unregulated transactions were producer or pipeline retail sales to industrial consumers or producer sales to pipelines within the states where gas was produced.[10]

The mission of first the Federal Power Commission and then the Federal Energy Regulatory Commission was to hold prices down and increase service coverage for the benefit of consumers of gas. Prices in excess of direct costs of services, at any level of the industry, was exploitation of the consumer by that source of supply. In the *Phillips* decision the Court stated: "Regulation of the sales in interstate commerce for resale made by a so-called independent natural gas producer is not essentially different from regulation of such sales when made by an affiliate of an interstate pipeline company. In both cases, the rates charged may have a direct and substantial effect on the price paid by the ultimate consumers. Protection of consumers against exploitation at the hands of natural gas companies was the primary aim of the Natural Gas Act."[11]

This conception does not *necessarily* conflict with additional goals of enhancing efficiency in use of resources for the long-term benefit of the consumer. "Preventing exploitation" is consistent with limiting prices of monopoly service providers at the wellhead, or in long distance transportation, or in final distribution beyond the city gate. Increasing the accessibility and reliability of service improves product quality and stimulates consumer demand.

INITIAL PRICE CONTROL

Given the history of, and the mandate for, wellhead regulation, the Federal Power Commission initially was committed to holding prices at levels related to "costs of service" however defined and measured. In fact, elaborate procedures were established for determining costs based on accounting outlays and on expert opinions on required rates of return. The producer was treated as if it had market power to set prices, and the commission procedures for limiting prices centered on case-by-case decision making. The commission authorized the companies one by one to set prices so that operating earnings were sufficient to recover the historical costs of investments, interpreting the Natural Gas Act, which required it to "investigate and ascertain the actual legitimate cost of the property of every natural gas company, the depreciation therein, and, when found necessary for rate-making purposes, other facts which bear on the determination of the fair value of such property."[12]

Case-by-case determination of the allowed price levels on contract wellhead production in a field proved to be problematic.[13] Even if price limits set by this process were to succeed in generating sufficient revenues to recover costs, at least two crippling problems emerged. First, there were too many producers, and too many contracts of each producer, to apply administratively this case-by-case price control procedure. Second, gas production was not subject to technical conditions in which producers individually could set prices. Prices based on individual costs made no economic sense. In fact, cost increases in some field areas were negative, because later new discoveries of gas in that field reduced extensive drilling and resulted in higher production per existing well.[14] As time passed, producers found additional supplies that required additional investment for the same rate of contract production, which on the margin came to more than historical cost.[15] Under this price control regime, older reserves would have lower, even negative prices, whereas newer reserves would have higher prices, all in the same market.

The Federal Power Commission attempted to ensure supply by requiring that pipelines contract for enough gas to fill the capacity of their systems at peak periods. This practice was applied to transporters over the 1950s and 1960s so that, prospectively, the future demands for gas by distributors and large industrial users would be satisfied. As this system evolved, regulation became more embedded in contract terms and conditions. The commission not only approved "just and reasonable" rates but whether service was "necessary." After the Supreme Court *Phillips* decision of 1954, the "reasonable" tests were applied to wellhead contracts. But production from reserve horizons varied, not only with the business cycle and the weather but with a wide range of geological conditions. No two contracts had similar costs, so that each transaction required the equivalent of a full-blown certificate and rate case.[16]

Moreover, the regulated wellhead contract became exceedingly complex. It called for production out of proved reserves over a five- to twenty-five-year period. With a term this lengthy, clauses were inserted to prevent delivery conditions in the future from departing from conditions in the market in that future period; they began to include take-or-pay clauses that required payments to be made on the basis of a take rate, regardless of whether gas was produced. Producers were protected from making premature commitments by most-favored-nation clauses (MFN), which required pipelines to pay prices that prevailed on later new contracts for reserves in adjoining fields or reservoirs. These terms were approved by the FPC.

FIELD GAS PRICE REGULATION IN THE 1970S

Across the country, gas retail and wholesale markets experienced substantial shortages in the mid-1970s. Shortages were manifest in service curtailments for interruptible customers and in refusals to connect new firm service customers. According to the commission, interstate gas distributors were 3 percent short of meeting demands of municipal retailers and industrial buyers in 1971 but 10 percent short of meeting these demands in 1974. In that period, the FPC staff forecast that the shortage would grow to be as large as 20 percent of demands by 1980.[17]

Consumers in some regions of the country fared worse in obtaining gas than those in other regions. Buyers in the North Central region, the Northeast, and on the West Coast, in that order, incurred most of the shortage. New residential buyers and new as well as some old industrial buyers in those three regions were cut off by local distribution systems from 1973 to the end of the winter of 1976–1977. In the North Central region this curtailment comprised as much as one half of demands, so that nearly all industrial and commercial establishments on gas systems experienced some elimination of service. In the other regions, where industry was not cut off entirely, industrial buyers seeking to expand uses of gas were unable to do so with supplies from the interstate pipelines.

At the same time, however, buyers in the South could still obtain the supply they sought by locating their activities within one of the producing states. They did so in significant numbers, increasing regional industrial development and reorienting gas production and distribution systems toward local consumption in the South and Southwest. Their purchases were not sales for resale in interstate commerce and thus were not subject to FPC price controls.

The gas shortage generated numerous public policy issues. Customers asked why there was a shortage, how long it would last, and if the shortage could be dealt with by the federal regulatory agency responsible for security of supply. The answers involve comparing the behavior of field markets under regulatory controls with that in the same markets assuming that there were no such controls. Price and production differences from these two scenarios show the effects of controls; they give blame to the regulators for the shortage.

The comparison begins with discussion of the process of developing reserves for production in the 1970s. Field markets for natural gas center on transactions in which producing companies dedicate newly discovered *reserves* to be used for *production* injected into pipeline transmission lines. The producing companies initiate the discovery process by seismic logging and well drilling to "prove out" new gas deposits. They make gas available for sale by drilling development wells; when sold as dedicated reserves, it is brought to the surface, where water, sulfur, and liquid by-products are removed. The gas is then injected into pipelines for transmission to wholesale industrial users or retail distributing companies that in turn deliver to households, commercial establishments, or retail industrial users. Forty-five percent of the natural gas production ends up delivered to residential and commercial consumers for heating and cooking, while 55 percent is consumed as boiler fuel or process material in industry.[18]

Gas reserves are accumulated through a process beginning with determining that there are in-ground deposits of (1) "associated" gas in crude oil formations and (2) "nonassociated" gas in "dry" or "wet" formations. They come about from new discoveries or from extensions or revisions of previous discoveries (extensions from beyond the limits of known fields and revisions from within known fields). They are dedicated in contracts calling for production over a five- to twenty-five-year period. These reserves are not known for certain and are changed by extensions and revisions, so that contracts are no more than agreements to deliver in the future an amount supported by an estimate.

The process of adding to reserves begins some years before commitments are made to pipelines. The producers' geophysical exploratory work shows the existence of a potential in-ground hydrocarbon reservoir; wells are drilled into the reservoir to determine the extent of that producing horizon. Geophysical work and wells are both investments under uncertainty that, with increased information, become increasingly more certain in physical product. But both exploratory and development wells depend upon expected future prices that, if high, lead to more activity and subsequently to more reserves for contract commitment. And prices are not the only determinant of the volume of reserves. Given that there is a fixed inventory of in-ground gas discovered, technical advancements in geophysical and production processes make it feasible to find more of the smaller and less accessible volumes so that the discoveries increase even at constant prices.

This process provides perspective on the condition of reserves and production at the time of the shortage. At that time, in the mid-1970s, the limit on *total reserves* did not appear to be constraining. We were not "out" of discoverable reserves in the United States. The sum total of past production and of present reserves totaled 640 tcf, less than 40 percent of the amount of ultimate discoverable reserves expected to be found by even cautious forecasters.[19] But there were limits on production out of contracted reserves. The time profile of production under existing contracts depended on a number of geological, engineering, and economic factors. Production could not take place physically at rates greater than a certain percentage of committed reserves (that is, the reservoir was so formed that the gas could not move to the wellhead at more than a certain "maximum efficient rate"). Production out of dedicated reserves at that time was at limits given by these technical factors.

Gas field price regulation fundamentals. For the first decade the FPC attempted to respond to the *Phillips* mandate with a price control process applied to contracts in the *Phillips* case itself, since that case had been remanded by the court for a finding of "just and reasonable" prices. The commission used "cost of service" methodology to find in that case that "just and reasonable" prices were higher than the original prices objected to by the state of Wisconsin. During the years that the commission dealt with *Phillips,* other companies filed more than 2,900 applications for price review. The resulting queue was soon so long that the commission forecast that it would not finish its 1960 caseload until the year 2043. The administrative crisis created by treating each of thousands of contracts as if they were single rate cases made it necessary to find other ways of regulating field prices.[20]

The FPC then developed a generic process for setting ceiling prices on all contracts within a producing region. The first step was to freeze any new contract price at the average price established on all contracts the previous year. In 1965 to 1970 this resulted in new contract prices capped at the 1965 annual average. The freeze was to be temporary, and followed by "area rate" cases that would set permanent basin-area maximum prices. In the area proceedings, the to-be-allowed rates were based on average costs of gas then being produced in that region; indeed, considerable attention in the first three proceedings was given to calculating specific region production costs, investment costs and allowable rates of return.

This new approach turned out to be fraught with strategic error. The commission was basing maximum price on historical costs. But cost estimates from the previous year were from operations when temporary price ceilings were in effect. If producers were rational, and undertook projects only when their costs were less than ceiling prices, then historical costs were determined by the temporary ceiling prices. The commission found that test-period development and production costs per mcf were in line with the temporary ceilings, and then determined that permanent rate ceilings should hold at the level of these costs. Temporary ceilings determined historical costs that set permanent ceilings.

Circular or not, area rate proceedings maintained the price level.[21] The courts approved, finding that price increases were to be denied because they were increases, as exemplified by *Atlantic Refining Company v. Public Service Commission* (360 U.S. 378), where price increases were denied because they were "greatly in excess of that which Tennessee pays from any lease in southern Louisiana."[22] The commission intended to "hold the line against increases in natural gas prices, which was consistent with its mandate."[23]

The result was a constant price level on new contracts for gas going to the interstate pipelines during the 1960s. The commission succeeded in holding gas prices steady while prices of other fuels were increasing. The volume-weighted average new contract price was 18.2 cents per thousand cubic feet in 1961, and 19.8 cents per thousand cubic feet in 1969.[24] Average wellhead prices on all contracts increased from 16.4 cents to 17.5 cents per mcf from 1961 to 1969, mostly as a result of the replacement of the oldest contracts at lower prices with new contracts at the average price level. These prices when passed through to buyers with the transportation markup resulted in a wholesale price of 32.0 cents per million Btu in 1962 and 33.4 cents per million Btu in 1970. At the same time prices for #2 fuel oil at wholesale increased from 34.5 cents to 39.8 cents and for industrial contract coal in large volume from 25.6 cents to 31.2 cents per million Btu.[25]

By 1970–1971, there were significant reductions in discovered reserves and in those reserves under contract to the interstate pipelines. In response, the commission made changes in its practices to allow the pipelines to attract more reserves away from local markets not subject to price controls. Area rate decisions increased the level of field prices based on "recognizing the urgent need for increased gas exploration and much larger annual reserve additions to maintain adequate service." The FPC "offered producers several price incentives," in those basin areas containing more than 85 percent of the reserves going into interstate production, including price increases of 3.0 cents per thousand cubic feet (in Kansas) to 5.2 cents per thousand cubic feet (in southern Louisiana) on new contracts.[26] The commission also began a new proceeding (Docket R389A) to set a national ceiling price on all new contracts, with the intention of providing a substantial price increase (as indicated by its decision at that time to allow rates in the Rocky Mountain area to increase by 7.0 cents per mcf).[27] It began to certify prices for new contract gas above the permanent area ceilings when it was "shown to be in the public interest."[28]

The results of these changes were real increases in wellhead new contract prices. The average new contract price increased from 19.8 cents per mcf in 1969 to 33.6 cents per mcf in 1972 and to 36 cents per mcf in 1973. In effect, new contract prices increased by 70 percent in four years. Market responses determined whether this was too little and too late to prevent the development of shortages of reserves and production over the rest of the decade. The responses of supply were slow to develop, as will be seen.

Whether this was "good regulation" depended, however, both on the rationale to regulate gas producers and on the results achieved in pursuit of the rationale. Upon reflection, it appears that there were two conceptually distinct purposes, and neither the agency nor the courts took pains to distinguish between them.

The first purpose was to control "market power." Restraint of market power is a traditional rationale; stated in direct terms, where only few companies provide the product to a market, they collectively can restrict supply so that the volume is less than would be provided in competition. The few firms restrict output to increase price, given that higher prices are more profitable. Such monopolistic tendencies can be controverted through price regulation by a regulatory commission. The purpose of regulation of gas distributors and interstate pipelines was to constrain market power of one or few providers to raise prices. Supporters of producer regulation advanced the same rationale for price controls on gas sales at the wellhead. Some asserted that gas production was concentrated in a few companies that controlled the supply of gas to the large interstate pipelines.[29] And their argument went further: unless market power at the wellhead was checked, pipeline regulation could not be effective. Monopoly prices for gas at the wellhead paid by pipelines would be passed through the "weighted average cost of gas" in the merchant service package to retail distributors and then to final consumers. In the words of the Supreme Court, "The rates charged [by producers] have a direct and substantial effect upon the price paid by the ultimate consumers. Protection of consumers against exploitation at the hands of natural gas companies was the primary aim of the Natural Gas Act."[30]

But this argument asserting the need to check "producer market power" played a diminished role in the FPC in the 1960s debate over price caps on wellhead reserve contracts. The evidence as to concentration in supply, in terms of the number of important sources of new contract reserves, did not support the assertion that there were "few" providers. Rather, ownership of reserves was as widely dispersed as production capacity in most manufacturing industries, which were not subject to that argument for regulation. As the Fifth Circuit Court of Appeals finally pointed out, "There seems to be general agreement that the market is at least structurally competitive."[31]

The most revealing indicator of market power, if it existed, would have been a high level of concentration in newly contracted-for gas reserves. But the commission statistics indicated that in defined (basin-wide) markets in the 1960s, the four largest gas producers accounted for less than 10 percent, and the fifteen largest producers accounted for less than 50 percent, of new reserves across any producing basin.[32] Supply was not highly concentrated even when the market definition of a basin was only a few hundred miles across. In the Permian Basin of West Texas and adjoining New Mexico, for example, the five largest producers accounted for somewhat less than 50 percent of new reserves.[33] Commenting on similar dispersion for county-sized basins, M. A. Adelman characterized this degree of concentration as "low," in fact "lower than 75–85 percent of [industries in] manufactured products"; and James McKie stated that entry into any basin is so unimpeded that even if concentration were much higher the largest producers would not be able to charge higher than competitive prices.[34]

The rejoinder was that the relevant market was for all reserves but that prices were being leveraged by the new contract price in a very thin market for new reserves. A few producers were "able" to raise prices on new contracts that were then passed on to old contracts by favored nations clauses in these old contracts.[35] This argument, however, also had little basis in prevalent conditions in gas markets. The four largest companies provided from 37 to 44 percent of new reserve contract volume in West Texas and 26 to 28 percent in the Texas Gulf region in the period just before the *Phillips* decision. These levels of concentration in new reserves were all less than half the concentration in demands for new reserves of the four largest pipeline buyers in these regions. Power to control new contract prices was probably limited, but if there was not "a balance," then the ability to set prices too low lay with the pipelines rather than the ability to set prices too high with the producers.[36]

Of course, one could still argue that, despite its apparently competitive structure, the producing segment of the industry behaved noncompetitively. Certain proponents of regulation, such as some of the gas distributing companies in the 1960s, asserted that the rapid rise in the field price of natural gas between 1950 and 1958 was evidence of noncompetitive performance (prices rose from 9 cents per mcf to 24 cents per mcf in the Gulf Coast region, on average, for example). More comprehensive analyses of markets for new contracts indicate that noncompetitive producer behavior did not cause price increases; rather, price increases followed from the pipelines losing the power to exact (monopsony) prices in new gas contracts. The 1950s prices for reserves were below competitive levels because of the lack of competition on the purchase side of markets. During the early 1960s, several pipelines sought reserves in field locations where previously there had been a single pipeline, and their entry raised new contract prices to 20-cent-plus levels. Competition among buyers—that is, incumbent and entering pipelines—not lack of competition among sellers, accounted for price increases that were said to prove "the need" for seller regulation.[37]

Proponents of regulation also argued that competition was negligible because the pipelines had no incentive to bargain for prices as low as competitive levels. Because the resale of gas by the pipeline companies was regulated on the basis of the purchase costs plus transportation costs in the merchant contract of the pipelines, then these pipelines, instead of resisting, simply passed purchase-price gas increases on to the retailer. This "passing on" argument fails to take account of limits on price increases in the merchant contract that reduce total throughput. The regulated firm prefers higher throughput on which a rate of return on transportation costs would be earned.[38] And the evidence suggests that pipelines in fact bargained for prices. In the 1950s, pipelines pushed field prices below competitive levels, and when the low price threatened to drive producers out of exploration and development, rather than increase their purchase-price offers to producers, the pipelines went into the exploration business themselves. They selectively produced higher-cost gas while continuing to pay low (monopsony) prices for the low-cost gas from the producing companies, so as to reduce their outlays.[39]

In addition to conjectures about lack of supplier competition, supporters of field price regulation pointed to supplier "profits" as evidence that price controls were necessary. In fact, earnings after interests and taxes appeared to be high in comparison with manufacturing industries. Economic witnesses appearing for the distributing companies in the Permian Basin Area Rate Proceeding reported average returns on capital between 12 and 18 percent for gas-producing companies in that basin, at a time when the average return in manufacturing was less than 8 percent. This comparison, however, did not establish the existence of monopoly pricing, given two special features of returns in the gas-producing industry. First, these companies comprised a sample of those with high discovery rates in a population that included many more companies who were experiencing exploratory failure. The high returns were those of firms still in business and not those with dry holes. With seven of eight exploratory wells coming out dry in the early years, company failure rates were high; and calculating industry returns based on those of surviving companies resulted in average returns biased on the high side. Second, returns were calculated by dividing the total profits that producers reported by the total capital that they reported, overlooking the extensive time lag between investment and when it begins to earn a return. Producer witnesses in the Permian Basin Area Rate Proceeding estimated that an apparent yield of 16 to 18 percent was equivalent, because of the lag, to a "true" yield of 10 percent.

Arguments to the effect that competition did not exist in gas production in the 1960s were probably wrong. The implications for policy based on this incorrect argument could be highly adverse. If producers lacked market power, regulating them as though they had such power does nothing but disrupt markets. The FPC, acting on the monopoly rationale when it did not apply, had to push prices below the competitive level if it were to decree any price below the one that it found in the contracts. Those paying lower than the competitive price would use this fuel more intensively even though the economy could provide other fuels that would be relatively more efficient. The lower price would reduce incentives to supply new reserves, given that returns to producers at the margin would be negative. By increasing the quantity demanded, and decreasing the quantity supplied, regulatory price ceilings could cause shortages.

The second recurring rationale for field price regulation was that it was necessary to contain windfall profits. Even in a competitive market, it was argued, a few suppliers making large discoveries realize profit returns that are unacceptable. These producers realize economic rents—that is, returns in excess of those required to bring forth production; they should be required to charge less for their production.

Although no one ever estimated the rents that gas producers would have earned without regulation during the 1960s, there is reason to believe that they would have been large compared to those in other industries. For one, reserves in the ground in large quantities were almost wholly lacking until extensive exploration and development was completed. The competitive market price of gas production would be in line with the cost of marginal additional exploration and development of reserves. As the reserve base expanded and the best deposits were tapped, then low-cost supplies were replaced by higher-cost supplies. The difference between price levels of new supplies and average production costs of old and new supplies was an appreciable rent to all producers.

Proponents of regulation sought to eliminate the price-cost differences on old reserves in established contracts, without interfering with decisions to undertake the discovery of new reserves. To do so, they had to hold down the price of old reserves while allowing high prices for marginal new reserves. That is, regulation had to set separate prices for old and new sources of supply that would result in excess demands for lower-priced old reserves. Where the primary aim was to redistribute the rental gains of producers to consumers, the secondary aim was to set out a regulatory process on prices that operated *without* affecting production.

The Federal Power Commission never distinguished between objectives of controlling market power and transferring rents. The commission early on issued statements that indicated it was trying to achieve both, but in later years, there was a shift toward the second objective, after it acknowledged that its efforts to cap prices had reduced reserves and production. Lowering prices from "monopoly" to "competitive" levels should have had the opposite effect, increasing both reserves and production until price was equal to marginal costs. The commission's subsequent efforts to cap prices made it clear that it was not trying to control monopoly power, and its decision to set two price levels in the area rate proceedings with higher prices on "new" gas and lower prices on "old" gas, made it clear that it was trying to take economic rents out of competitive supply.[40] The commission's concern as to whether the two-level prices would be high enough, though limiting producer profits, moved it further from arguments that it was constraining monopoly power.[41]

The resulting behavior of field and resale markets. The commission price-cap process, by preventing price increases throughout the 1960s, created conditions highly conducive to the emergence of shortages in the 1970s. The freeze in prices brought about reductions in exploratory activity that reduced new reserves under regulation in the 1970s from 19 tcf to 10 tcf. This decline would not have occurred if new contract field prices had been higher in the earlier period. The difference is indicated by the behavior of the supply-and-demand model when one assumes the absence of the price-level freeze. Prices that cleared markets, as in figure 3.1, would have been twice the actual levels from 1968 to 1971, which would have increased reserves by 5 to 10 tcf per each year, enough to prevent the drawing down of the reserve stock, as illustrated in figure 3.2.[42]

At the same time that there were these limited increases in production, demands were increasing rapidly. The pipeline companies, which determined rates of take in contracts for reserves, increased these rates to full-capacity levels. The alternative was that they would have offered new customers or old customers with increased demands more throughput at the previous reserve-production ratio by amounts taken from an increased reserve inventory (model simulations for the early 1970s show levels from 2 to 4 tcf per year more 1968 to

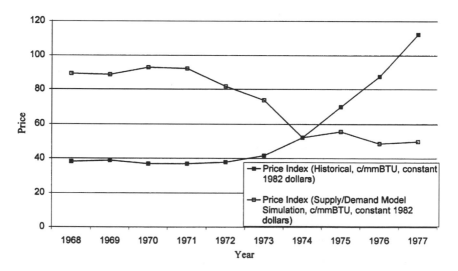

Figure 3.1. The price of gas, 1968–1977

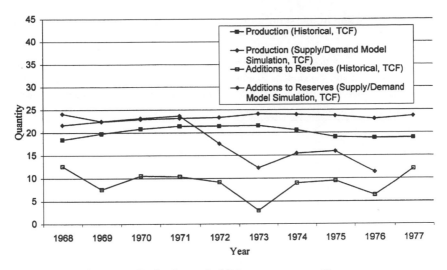

Figure 3.2. Production and additions to reserves, 1968–1977

1977 as in table 3.1 and as illustrated in figure 3.2). All that would have been required was a price level 50 cents per mcf higher than the regulated price level (as for P^*, the market clearing level, in table 3.1).

But what actually took place was that existing reserve inventories were reduced by increasing production and by decreasing additions to new reserve inventories at the capped prices. Increases in demands called for production increases from more new reserves than could be added.

Production varied from 21 to 19 tcf through the mid-1970s; production without controls would have increased to 23 tcf (as in column 2 of table 3.1). The price ceilings imposed by the commission reduced the additions to reserves, which was followed subsequently by stagnation in production. Demands were satisfied by increasing production out of previously committed reserves.[43]

The redistribution of reserves to immediate rather than future production made it difficult in 1970 to conclude that customers were benefiting from price controls. But by the mid-1970s almost all customers in the Northeast, the North Central region, and the West received less production as compared to those in the Southeast. By then, increased demands were being met by production out of old reserves, so that, in effect, reserve backing for continued service to established customers at the end of the regulated pipeline and distributor network was being used to meet additional demands of new customers outside the regulated network. Those losing the reserve backing were incumbent cus-

Table 3.1. Historical and model simulation prices, quantities, and reserves

Year	Production (historical, tcf)	Production (supply-demand model simulation, tcf)	Reserves (historical, tcf)	Reserves (supply-demand model simulation, tcf)	Price index (historical c/mmBtu constant 1982 dollars)	P* (model simulation, c/mmBtu constant 1982 dollars)
1968	18.49	21.71	293.19	337.78	38.24	89.36
1969	19.83	22.47	287.35	340.25	38.90	88.78
1970	20.87	22.97	275.11	340.32	36.92	92.94
1971	21.47	23.21	264.82	340.54	36.92	92.28
1972	21.49	23.39	253.75	341.04	37.88	81.80
1973	21.59	24.13	241.45	335.28	41.68	73.82
1974	20.58	23.99	222.81	323.43	52.13	52.22
1975	19.08	23.73	211.22	314.91	69.92	55.58
1976	18.87	23.06	201.63	307.12	87.57	48.64
1977	18.94	23.69	189.14	295.47	112.28	49.85

Sources: DOE/EIA historical statistics; DOE/EIA 1996; model simulations that establish equilibrium unregulated price index and quantity, as explained in the text.

Notes: [1] In chained 1982 cents, calculated using GDP Implicit Price Deflators.
[2] Converted from c/mcf to c/mmBtu using dry production heat content.
[3] Represents price of gas sold and delivered by local distribution companies and does not reflect gas transported for the others.
[4] Reserves are at beginning of year.

tomers under regulation, whereas those gaining were new customers being induced at least in part by low prices to expand their demands outside regulation.

What then can be concluded as to the gains and losses from wellhead price regulation? The gainers were customers paying lower prices for service received in the first half of the decade. The losers were customers taking a reduction in reserve backing and ending up without service at the end of the decade. The gains of those consumers who received production can be estimated using the model "market clearing" price P^*, the historical price P_h, and the historical quantity of production Q_h (see figure 3.3). These gains equal the difference in prices $(P^* - P_h)$ multiplied by production Q_h, in dollar terms equal to the area of the rectangle A in figure 3.3. For each year over the period from 1968 to 1977, for consumers for whom regulation successfully held down prices, these gains constitute loss for producers, because producers have had their prices reduced by that amount, with consequent cash-flow losses of A dollars per annum.

The losses of consumers doing without production equal half the difference

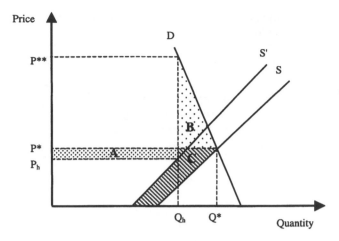

Figure 3.3. Gains and losses due to regulation

between the prices they would have paid $(P^{**} - P^*)$ for the gas they did not receive (equal to $Q^* - Q_h$) as indicated by the area of triangle B in figure 3.3.[44] Added to these losses are those of producers of returns from production forgone because of low prices, as depicted by the area between the supply curves, with and without regulation (the area C in figure 3.3).

The order of magnitude of total gains and losses is impressive. Consumers that received service had a total of more than $38 billion in benefits in the ten years from 1968 to 1977 (as in table 3.2). What they gained, producers lost, and more. Producer losses exceeded consumer gains by six billion dollars due to decreased production (in table 3.2, for area C). Their losses, which would have gone into returns to stockholders of gas producing companies, or into investment in exploration and development, played a role in generating changes in forthcoming exploration and development by the end of the decade. The large losers were consumers that could not get on the delivery system or that were partially curtailed in service. Their losses were more than $51 billion, almost 60 percent more than the gains of those consumers that did receive the gas they demanded. The price control process of the Federal Power Commission benefited some consumers with low-priced gas, but it inflicted greater losses on other consumers without gas. Buyers as a group as well as producers as a group lost by more than $20 billion over the ten-year period.

Thus the FPC, given the task of regulating gas field prices by the Supreme Court, after first trying to adapt utility regulatory techniques to set individual contract prices for new and old reserves at the wellhead, then went to area-wide

Table 3.2. Gains and losses of producers and customers as affected
by field price regulation

	Method of estimation	Estimated 1982 dollars (in millions)
Gains of customers who received actual production at lower regulated prices. Losses of producers at the same lower prices.	Difference between regulated and market clearing prices multiplied by historical production. (Area *A*)	38,687
Losses of producers reducing production because of lower regulated prices.	Decreased production times decreased prices divided by two. (Area *C*)	6,855
Losses of customers doing without production due to shortage.	Difference between regulated (historical) price and the market clearing price multiplied by the difference between regulated and market clearing production, divided by two. (Area *B*)	51,869

Source: As explained in the text and as derived from supply-demand model simulations.
Note: Aggregated, but not discounted, over the years 1968–1977.

price ceilings, only to fail on both applications. The commission's resolve to freeze prices was strengthened by court decisions stressing that it could determine prices using whatever review process that produced "reasonable" results. As caseloads caused congestion in the process, the commission's response in the area rate proceedings allowed it to put in place limits on prices over all contracts at one time that seemed reasonable. But although this achieved price stability, the commission's policies led to deficiencies in reserves and, ultimately, in gas production.

In the absence of controls, prices would have increased beyond the freeze level and thus maintained reserve-production ratios, expanded production, and held back demand growth. In the presence of controls, the commission process decreased reserve-production levels, reduced production-enhanced demand growth, and thus created shortages.

Based on these results the rationale for regulation can be reassessed. Even though the courts and the commission were never explicit as to who should receive benefits from this regulation, it can be assumed that those who actually did benefit were meant to be the recipients. Even so, assuming such does not lead to a conclusion that the regulation was effective. Consumers that had locked-in supplies benefited from fixed prices; but they lost the reserve backing for their production, because old reserves were used to provide expanded production for other consumers, some of whom were induced into the market only because of the low regulated prices. Consumers not so favored lost from not being able to obtain service, and they lost $13 billion more than the gains of those favored by having production.

The straightforward rationale for regulation was that it generated benefits from lower prices. The shortage, then, was not the intended result, given that those who did without experienced losses that were larger than these benefits. Nor could the rationale have been to reduce monopoly exploitation by producers; producers lost $44 billion, but their losses were not justified by consumer gains that should have followed from taking monopoly prices to lower levels.

THE NATURAL GAS POLICY ACT OF 1978
AS PARTIAL DEREGULATION OF FIELD GAS
SUPPLY MARKETS

Natural gas legislation in 1978 was a yearlong undertaking of the energy subcommittees of the House and Senate, of a House-Senate Conference Committee, and of the Office of the President. The resulting Natural Gas Policy Act was a building block in the Carter administration's program to make the country less vulnerable to interruptions of energy supply.[45] Gas supplies were short, and the intention was to eliminate shortages. Yet the goals of the NGPA went beyond clearing gas markets of excess demands spilling over into fuel oil markets. It had to prevent the producer of old contract reserves from benefiting from any nationwide gas price increases. The specter of monopoly was present in the call of the *New Republic* to the defense of the consumer: "The great gas compromise consecrated with a fanfare on May 24th may prove to be one of the lesser achievements of the 95th Congress. It was not a compromise at all but rather a defeat for the buyers of natural gas . . . [and] a defeat for the federal government in that it set a date certain for the government to surrender its power to control the price of natural gas. In the future, if this compromise is enacted, that power will rest exclusively with the gas companies."[46] But for

consumers with shortages, *Harper's* made the opposite call: "Government in-
volvement in natural gas pricing has been a disaster. It is particularly discourag-
ing to consider how much larger the natural gas market might have grown if
rigid price controls . . . had not been in place, resulting frequently in the shun-
ning of new gas customers."[47] The NGPA had to achieve the goals of both the
New Republic and *Harper's* by eliminating shortages without increasing prices
to those with existing supplies.

How any legislation could possibly achieve that much was unclear; even so,
the proponents of the NGPA laid down absolute requirements. The act had to
phase out area rate ceilings in order to eliminate shortages. It was recognized
that rate controls at the wellhead on additional reserves and production had to
be removed if there were going to be increases in production necessary to clear
markets. But follow-on adjustments of regulated prices at the city gate during
the transition to the end of shortages had to be made "equitable." The regulatory process had to prevent price increases to final consumers at the burner tip
as much as possible. Wellhead price increases on new contracts had to be "rolled
in" to the average wellhead price on old contracts. The old contract price would
be maintained and then passed on in the merchant service prices.

A new agency, the Federal Energy Regulatory Commission of the new Department of Energy, was to implement these pricing requirements. The price
adjustment process in place before the NGPA set the framework. By the middle 1970s, the Federal Power Commission had increased area rates. FPC Decision 770A adopted "forward-looking" and "comparative" production costs that
justified area rates from $0.50 to $1.42 per mcf on new contract gas. At the same
time, "emergency" federal legislation allowed industrial and commercial consumers in the North that were short of gas to buy in intrastate markets for shipment on their own account in the interstate pipelines at any price. This set of
initiatives raised prices on sales to industrial consumers to parity with wholesale
prices to retail distributors and reduced excess-demand pressures, but was in-
sufficient to cut into the most recent and most severe 1976–1977 consumer
shortages.

The NGPA was a compromise that came about in consolidating House and
Senate bills. The House sought to reduce the interstate gas shortages by making
regulation more comprehensive, so as to include intrastate sales, and then moving intrastate supplies to interstate markets. The Senate sought to deregulate
prices in interstate wellhead contracts. This contradiction was resolved in conference by phasing out price controls only on sources of additional supply, and

extending the phasing over substantial periods of time. As the House-Senate Conference Committee indicated: "Agreement reconciles two very different bills by redefining what qualifies as new natural gas and only deregulating the price of that gas."[48]

This elaborate process of "deregulation" applied both to new supplies and to supplies shifted from intrastate into interstate markets. It applied to deep but not shallow gas, at least not to the same extent; for example, for onshore new reserves: "Natural gas from new onshore production wells deeper than 5,000 feet is deregulated effective January 1, 1985, provided that such gas was not committed or dedicated to interstate commerce on April 20, 1977. Natural gas produced from new onshore production wells from a completion location shallower than 5,000 feet that was not dedicated to interstate commerce on April 20, 1977, is deregulated effective July 1, 1987, or as of the last date on which price controls are in effect if reimposed, whichever is later. Gas produced from new onshore production wells committed or dedicated to interstate commerce on April 20, 1977, is not deregulated."[49]

The act defined more than thirty classifications of jurisdictional natural gas. Only three classifications involved production that would be allowed to sell at unregulated prices. The two quantitatively important categories were "new" and "high cost" gas, which came under four classifications based on depth and location of reserves and were deregulated.[50] The designation of other classes of production for continued regulation was in significant detail; for example, new deep production qualified for special development incentives but continued price control when at a depth greater than 5,000 feet; although this production was allowed to be priced higher than area rates, the schedule of prices was capped over an extended period.[51] Reserves "dedicated to interstate commerce before November 9, 1978," were price decontrolled only after six years and had price schedules that differed according to whether the gas was produced by small or large companies. Offshore new gas committed under contracts dated after April 20, 1977, was price decontrolled, whereas onshore new gas was decontrolled only if it came from wells 1,000 feet deeper than existing marker wells.[52]

Most current production was not classified to be subject to immediate price decontrol. The time sequence of authorized price increases under phasing allowed new gas prices to increase from $1.75 per mcf in 1977, by 3.5 percent per year more than inflation until 1981, and by 4.0 percent per year more than inflation thereafter until the end of 1984. Old gas under new contracts was to be priced at $1.45 per mcf until 1984. Altogether, these schedules implied that "equitable" prices would be roughly 50 percent higher by the mid-1980s than they had been in the mid-1970s but that "equitable" prices were capped.

There was a specific condition in the NGPA for passing on higher field prices in the merchant contract with gas retailers. Old gas under contract to the interstate pipelines was to be assigned for resale to residential consumers, with any remaining volumes allocated to commercial and industrial consumers. New gas was to go to industrial consumers. As old gas was depleted, residential consumers obtained further production at a price equal to the "rolled-in" average of that pipeline's field purchase prices.[53] Commercial and industrial consumers were to obtain additional supplies priced at "incremental" field purchase prices for new gas,[54] up to the Btu-equivalent fuel oil price (and any further price increase was then allocated to the rolled-in price schedule).[55]

Price deregulation consisted of a set of classifications for gas contracts subject to price changes according to schedule. What outcomes could have been expected? The range of forecasts in the 1970s was that decontrolled prices would not reach levels necessary to clear shortages before the mid-1980s.

The Department of Energy (DOE) forecast was that with NGPA-prescribed decontrol classifications on gas prices and economy-wide inflation of 5 percent per annum, the average U.S. residential gas price would increase about 6 percent per year in current dollars for the next seven years. The price of gas to commercial and industrial buyers, with incremental pricing constrained by the fuel oil price, would rise by 9 percent per year.[56] Industrial demand would decrease by one third, and production supply would increase by one-fifth, so that shortages would be reduced by one half the level that could be expected under continued regulation over that period.

The American Gas Association econometric model predicted that excess demands would increase by 20 percent under the NGPA because supplies would actually be reduced. Conventional gas supply would fall short, because equivalent petroleum products prices of less than $5.00 per mcf would set a limit on gas prices that would be too low to bring forth sufficient supplies to clear out excess demands. Supplies from Canada and Mexico would be available, however, to expand the total by 10 percent, and synthetic gas from coal would contribute 19 percent more, for a total increase of 29 percent. These volumes from outside the market would be more than sufficient to eliminate excess demands, based on prices of $5.00 per mcf for Canadian and Mexican gas and of $5.70–$6.50 for synthetic gas, both of which would be higher than Btu-equivalent fuel oil prices.

Even over this range of forecast outcomes there was agreement that the

NGPA would not eliminate the shortage of gas supplies from conventional sources. The NGPA would work to squeeze out only part of excess gas demands, given that it was not going to generate enough new supply in the unregulated market and not going to reduce demands by bringing old contract prices up to new-equivalent level. Growth in residential demands was to be met by regulatory-determined allocation of additional supplies only to residential consumers. Additional gas for regulated industrial consumers would be available only from the residual from these allocations to home consumers. With such limited supply increases, there would be continued shortages. But they might never be realized in the national gas market because industrial consumers would permanently switch to alternative fuels. Such were the expected results from this brand of phased deregulation.

The effects of the NGPA were quickly realized. During the first four years under the act, gas market performance improved significantly. The shortages of the mid-1970s were reduced so that there were only limited curtailments in peak-heating periods. There were no curtailments in the 1979–1980 winter or in succeeding winters. The pipelines, in conjunction with retail gas utilities, began adding new customers to delivery systems before the end of the 1970s.

Three market-driven changes can be given credit for this remarkable turnaround. First, interstate gas supplies increased by more than the increase in total production as a result of shifts of contract reserves from intrastate buyers to the interstate pipelines. Second, limited economic growth throughout the economy in the late 1970s and early 1980s constrained the growth of gas demand in the industrial and commercial sectors. Third, on the demand side, the Fuel Use Act of 1979 curtailed industrial demands by requiring that power plants not add to generation capacity with natural gas as the fuel source. With new capacity dedicated to coal and nuclear fuel–based generation, new gas demands in the power sector were reduced to low levels.

The NGPA schedule for phased price increases focused the reserve and production development process on the "high-cost" gas with deregulated prices. Pipelines with large percentages of old reserve(low-price) contracts could and did make high price offers for deregulated gas given that their low "weighted average cost of gas" (WACOG) could be passed through to wholesale buyers. That is, the "cushion" of regulated old contract prices made it possible for them to bid high prices for additional supplies being offered at market.[57] The resulting contracts for new reserves shifted supplies to the New England and West North Central regions and away from the Southwestern producing region because the "cushion" was greatest for the northern pipelines.

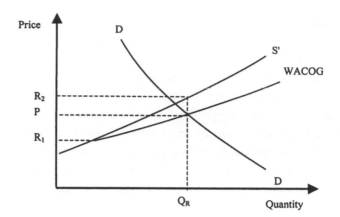

Figure 3.4. Partial deregulation in the long run

This process for escalating prices is indicated schematically in figure 3.4. The supply of deregulated gas, S', and of all gas at WACOG, raised the price from the regulated level R_1 to market-clearing P at which WACOG cleared demands Q_R. Those who obtain gas pay R_2 for new supplies not subject to price control; that price R_2 is rolled into the WACOG to be included in the average P. However, this is only the beginning of a dynamic process, as envisioned by the NGPA; as price control schedules on old gas run out and prices on new gas are deregulated, WACOG converges with S'. Then the price level R_2 results in excess supply by the difference between S' supply and D demand.

Not only were prices disoriented by the NGPA in this process, but regulated contract terms were distorted so that markets had to perform poorly. Contract terms become more favorable to the seller when prices are capped and gas is short; that is, buyers seek to lock in contract supply by offering conditions more favorable to the seller as a substitute for price increases that can't be offered. Take-or-pay provisions and price escalation in contracts are beneficial to sellers and burdensome to buyers. Given widely credited forecasts of continued shortages, the post-NGPA contracts reflected expectations of buyers that they could improve their position by making new contract commitments at regulated prices but with future price escalation conditions. As P. R. Carpenter, H. D. Jacoby, and A. W. Wright have observed, price escalation clauses were included in most new contracts signed in the late 1970s: "Even if the pipelines had wanted to hedge their bets, the intense competition for reserves would have made it difficult to get more flexible terms in new contracts. The excess demands coupled with peculiar incentives of the NGPA led the pipelines to bargain away flexibility in return for rights to reserves. Arguably, they had little choice: they had contractual service obligations to their customers. Inflexible contract provisions were to be expected in a seller's market."[58]

The results were observed by the commission and reported in a case involving Northern Natural Gas Company in July 1981:

> Because the ratio of reserves to market requirement of most major interstate pipelines declined significantly prior to the enactment of the NGPA, these pipelines were and are continually required to contract for new long-term gas supplies even though the immediate deliverability from those sources is not required by the pipeline's customers at present. Interstate pipelines contract for long-term supplies in the regulatory framework of the NGPA where some categories of gas production are completely deregulated while other categories remain subject to wellhead price regulation. As a result, interstate pipelines face fierce competition for price-controlled gas. Because the NGPA permits arms-length negotiations with respect to the non-price terms of producer contracts, this competition has resulted in interstate pipelines accepting and undertaking extensive take-or-pay obligations in connection with domestic gas supplies.[59]

The contracts signed during the period shortly after the NGPA went into effect developed that pattern of terms and conditions. Based on a survey that approximately four hundred producers filed with the Department of Energy "Natural Gas Producer/Pipeline Contract Report,"[60] the salient features were as shown in table 3.3. Ninety-five percent of these contracts were for terms of fifteen years or more. Price redetermination occurred at intervals of less than one year in 83 percent of 1981 contracts and 92 percent of 1982 contracts. The vast majority of contracts in 1981, 97 percent, had take-or-pay clauses for greater than 75 percent of deliverability. Moreover, the prevalence of take-or-pay clauses increased. As shown in table 3.4, the percentage of "required take" in contracts of pre-1973 vintage was in the range of 60 to 65 percent, but in contracts executed during the period 1973–1977 was 80 to 85 percent. For contracts executed after 1979, weighted-average percentage take requirements were in the range of 78 to 82 percent.

Considerable uncertainty remained, however, as to whether those escalating prices would prevail. If they did not, then the pipeline had to have "market-out" from the contract. "Market-out" provisions became more prevalent in 1981–1982 (see table 3.3). Of the 1981 contracts, only 36 percent included market-out provisions, but of the 1982 contracts, 85 percent had market-out clauses. The data do not indicate, however, the nature of the clauses contained in the contract sample, the conditions under which they could be exercised or

Table 3.3. Summary of major provisions in contracts filed at FERC, 1981–1982

	1981 (%)	1982 (%)
Contracts with terms for less than 15 years	5	3
Take-or-pay clauses requiring take greater than 75%	97	75
Price redetermination at an interval of 1 year or less	83	92
Require redetermination based on number 2 fuel oil price	36	47
Require redetermination based on number 6 fuel oil price	7	11
"Market-out" price provisions	36	85
Number of contracts	N = 41	N = 72

Source: DOE/EIA 1983.

whether they would provide alternative prices to work out the contract. Moreover, based on Form EIA-758 data, the Energy Information Agency of the DOE concluded that the likelihood of a market-out condition in a contract depended on the presence of other contract provisions. Those contracts that included most favored nations clauses and oil parity clauses had the lowest percentage of market-out clauses. And, as indicated in table 3.5, the prevalence of market-out clauses in contracts with both favored nations and gas and oil price parity clauses actually declined over the period 1979–1981. In 1979, 21.2 percent of the gas with both most favored nations and oil parity provisions came from contracts subject to market-out provisions, whereas in 1980 and 1981 this proportion declined to 18.2 percent and 13.4 percent, respectively. Most likely, contracts with all three conditions were not typical and were instead for commitments of reserves still in short supply to the few remaining pipelines with deliverability deficits. The other contracts signed in the early 1980s were to include provisions that gave the pipeline the right to suspend take of the gas if prices were higher than those in later contracts.

With these price and other conditions, then, how did the NGPA affect the interests of producers and consumers? Implementation of the NGPA began at a time when energy markets in general were marked by tight supply. The doubling of crude oil prices in 1978–1980 had created at least an impression that restriction of supply in world crude markets would dominate energy prices over the coming decade. The gas shortage was perceived to be extensive and would be eliminated only over the 1980s. In such a context, the NGPA would phase out price controls over six years or more and not eliminate gas shortages. Government and industry forecasters predicted that there would continue to be excess gas demand over the 1978–1984 period of "phasing" of price decontrol.

Table 3.4. Summary of take-or-pay provisions by vintage for 1980 and 1981
(based on percentage of deliverability or capacity)

Vintage	Weighted average percentage take requirement	Quantity (quadrillion Btu)	Average price ($/mmBtu)
1980			
Before 1973	59.6%	1.64	$1.49
1973–Apr. 20, 1977	85.9%	1.07	$2.33
Apr. 21, 1977–Nov. 8, 1977	82.3%	1.37	$2.22
Nov. 9, 1978–1979	82.5%	0.77	$2.49
After 1979	78.3%	0.54	$3.49
1981			
Before 1973	64.9%	1.76	$1.96
1973–Apr. 20, 1977	85.8%	0.86	$2.60
Apr. 21, 1977–Nov. 8, 1977	84.4%	1.73	$2.27
Nov. 9, 1978–1979	82.6%	0.95	$3.07
After 1979	81.8%	1.45	$4.14

Source: DOE/EIA 1983.

The prices negotiated in early post-NGPA new gas contracts free of controls reflected these conditions by escalating to $4 or more per mcf.

But market demands did not increase as predicted, and additional supplies were met with relatively stable demands in this period. The relatively slow growth of the economy held back increases in demands, as did fuel switching and gains in fuel-use efficiencies.[61] The interstate pipelines acquired new reserves almost immediately from extensive reallocations of intrastate supplies and from limited new discoveries, extensions, and revisions. The elimination of shortages was achieved two to five years earlier than the most optimistic forecasts.

Rapid changes in fuel oil markets had effects on this process. Increases in oil prices in the late 1970s, which were expected to result in increased gas demands, were followed by equally large declines in the early to mid-1980s: crude prices fell from $5.48 per mmBtu in 1981 to $2.18 per mmBtu in 1986, causing the heating oil price for industrial users competitive with gas to fall from $4.48 per mmBtu in 1981 to $2.51 per mmBtu in 1986 (see table 3.6).[62] These relative price decreases caused switching from gas to oil sources of energy, a process already initiated by the prohibitions against gas use in power plants.

Table 3.5. Trends in market-out provisions for post-NGPA contracts

Year of production—type of clause	Quantity with deregulation clauses (quadrillion Btu)	Percentage with market-out clauses
1979		
Most-favored nation	1.35	9.0%
Oil parity*	0.03	45.0%
Both	0.24	21.2%
Neither	0.51	13.4%
1980		
Most-favored nation	2.05	24.0%
Oil parity*	0.03	41.7%
Both	0.77	18.2%
Neither	0.86	16.3%
1981		
Most-favored nation	2.64	35.7%
Oil parity*	0.05	67.0%
Both	1.52	13.4%
Neither	1.04	41.3%

Source: DOE/EIA 1983.

Notes: 1981 data are partial year data extrapolated to full year.

*Results on market-out clauses based on five or fewer sampling units.

Table 3.6. Gas and heating oil prices to industrial consumers

Year	Gas price*	Change from previous year (%)	Heating oil price*	Change from previous year (%)	Gas price as percentage of heating oil price
1980	2.52	28.6	3.69	33.7	68.3
1981	3.07	21.8	4.48	21.4	68.5
1982	3.80	23.8	4.46	(0.4)	85.2
1983	4.10	7.9	4.38	(1.8)	93.6
1984	4.13	0.7	4.68	6.8	88.2
1985	3.87	(6.3)	4.24	(9.4)	91.3
1986	3.20	(17.3)	2.51	(40.8)	127.5
1987	2.88	(10.0)	2.87	14.3	100.3
1988	2.90	0.7	2.34	(18.5)	123.9
1989	2.93	1.0	2.75	17.5	106.5
1990	2.94	0.3	3.10	12.7	94.8

Source: DOE/EIA 1980–1990.

Note: *Prices are current dollars per million Btus.

Table 3.7. Natural gas consumption by sector (tcf)

Year	Residential	Commercial	Industrial	Electric utilities	Total
1980	4.75	2.61	8.20	3.68	19.88
1981	4.55	2.52	8.06	3.64	19.40
1982	4.63	2.61	6.94	3.23	18.00
1983	4.38	2.43	6.62	2.91	16.83
1984	4.56	2.52	7.23	3.11	17.95
1985	4.43	2.43	6.87	3.04	17.28
1986	4.31	2.32	6.50	2.60	16.22
1987	4.31	2.43	7.10	2.84	17.21
1988	4.63	2.67	7.48	2.64	18.03
1989	4.78	2.72	7.89	2.79	18.80
1990	4.41	2.67	8.39	2.78	18.83

Source: DOE/EIA 1990, table 77.

Natural gas consumption decreased for all classes of customers, by 18 percent from 1980 to 1986 (see table 3.7). The largest declines were in industrial (−20.7 percent) and utility demands (−29.3 percent), and the smaller declines were in home consumer demands (−9.3 percent).

In this context, the NGPA process, implemented by FERC, set ceilings on old contract prices and decontrolled certain new contract prices. Pipelines that bid for new contract gas reserves were limited only by the necessity that their weighted average cost of gas (WACOG) when passed on to retail buyers in the transport-gas package was in line with other fuel prices. Focused on long-term contracts, the NGPA ceiling and phasing process allowed WACOG to go to high levels.

Prices in contracts executed during the years 1978–1981 for reserves newly available from offshore blocks throughout the Gulf of Mexico and from on-shore fields in Louisiana are illustrative of those generally in deregulated transactions. The range of initial prices in contracts executed in 1979 was $2.15 to $3.50 per mmBtu (see table 3.9). In 1980 the range was from $1.75 to $4.50 per mmBtu, and in 1981 the range increased to from $2.29 to $6.00 per mmBtu. And these contracts contained escalation and renegotiation clauses that made it possible and, at the time, likely that there would be higher price levels for succeeding years.

By the early 1980s, gas delivery markets did not support these prices. High and increasing new contract prices pushing up the WACOG made wholesale

Table 3.8. Selected energy prices, 1982–1988 (1988 $/mcf)

Year	Spot gas	WACOG*	Long-term contract	Residual fuel oil
1982	n/a	3.73	n/a	6.29
1983	n/a	3.85	n/a	5.48
1984	3.33	3.57	3.36	5.64
1985	2.64	3.32	3.02	4.87
1986	1.72	2.78	2.05	2.76
1987	1.50	2.41	2.06	3.22
*1988***	1.60	2.19	2.68	2.55

Source: DOE/EIA 1989, table 15.
Notes: *Pipeline weighted average cost of gas.
**Third quarter (September) of 1988.

gas at city gates too high to be competitive with other industrial and commercial fuels (see table 3.6 for 1983–1989 for industrial fuel prices). As a consequence, reductions in wholesale demands led to lower rates of take of gas under contract by the interstate pipelines. Producers were prepared to provide, as early as 1983, more than 3 tcf more than pipelines would take. This so-called bubble in supply expanded to more than 4 tcf in the next two years. While estimates varied widely, depending on what producers stated were required take-or-pay rates, excess supply was 2 to 5 tcf per year (see table 3.10). Production of the bubble could still take place, however, if not under the pipeline long-term contracts. Spot sales off contract could be arranged at prices below contract in informal markets. Wholesale buyers went to nonpipeline sources of gas for un-

Table 3.9. Initial base price in Louisiana and offshore natural gas contracts, 1979–1981

Contract year	Contracts (N)	Minimum price	Average price	Median price	Maximum price
1979	10	$2.15	$2.49	$2.33	$3.50
1980	29	$1.75	$2.94	$2.59	$4.50
1981	24	$2.29	$3.41	$3.49	$6.00
Total	63				

Source: Foster Associates, 1979–1981.
Note: Prices are per mmBtu; includes all contracts with slated initial prices for Louisiana and offshore contracts.

Table 3.10. Estimates of natural gas surplus, 1982–1989 (tcf)

Year	AGA	Chase Manhattan Bank	*Oil and Gas Journal* surveys	Bankers Trust	Booz•Allen
1982	—	1.7	—	—	—
1983	—	3.2	<7	3.8	—
1984	3.2	—	2–4	—	—
1985	3.6	—	—	—	—
1986	2.6	—	—	—	4.5 (peak)
1987	—	—	—	—	—
1988	1.5	—	—	—	—
1989	0.85	—	—	—	—

Sources: "Chase Manhattan" 1984; "Bankers Trust" 1984; "OGJ Newsletter" 1985; "AGA" 1986; Booz•Allen, "Change, Uncertainty" 1988; AGA, "Weak Wellhead Prices" 1989.

bundled supplies at prices at least a dollar less than those for merchant gas at the WACOG (table 3.8).

By 1985, excess supply and resulting contract holdups had caused FERC to initiate a process that enabled pipelines to cash out long-term contracts. Gas owned by pipelines in the bubble of excess deliverability could be shifted into spot markets after a cash settlement. The gas then put into the spot market made up a significant percentage of that produced by the late 1980s, with 0.22 tcf of spot gas sold in 1982 increasing to 7.22 tcf sold in 1987,[63] accounting for approximately 55 percent of gas deliveries in 1987. Spot transactions took over by the early 1990s, accounting for more than 90 percent of pipeline transportation volumes by the second quarter of 1991.[64]

The NGPA results were thus in conflict with those originally expected of phased price-cap regulation. Prices in this regime were too high rather than too low. Even so, price above supply-and-demand equilibrium had the same effect as that below, that of reducing consumer gain below the level that would have been realized in the absence of regulation. By the end of this period there were two levels of production, the contract and spot levels. What producers gained in higher prices consumers lost, but what producers lost in having to dispose of surplus at spot prices was not made up in consumer gains. Thus, all participants in these markets were worse off as phased price decontrol worked through.

Gains and losses for producers and consumers due to the NGPA are shown in figure 3.5. Producers benefited from higher prices, with policy-generated increases shown by $P - P^*$, equal to the difference between NGPA and dereg-

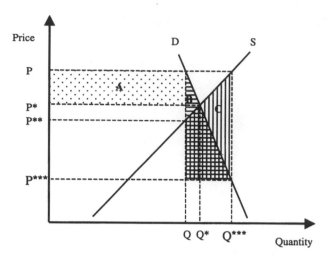

Figure 3.5. Gains and losses due to passage of the NGPA

ulated prices, on the quantity Q actually taken (area A). Consumers lost the same amount, given that they otherwise would have been able to take that quantity at the deregulated price P^* (area A). Producers also had losses from disposing of the surplus, equal to $Q^{***} - Q$, the difference between throughput available and actual pipeline take. Assuming that this surplus was put into spot sales, it is cleared out of markets at price P^{***}. The lower price causes losses to producers by selling all gas below marginal cost, the area under the supply curve (area C). Part of these losses are gains to consumers from being able to purchase the additional quantity at that low price (equal only to area B).

Estimates of these gains and losses are in tables 3.11 and 3.12. Production, prices, and revenues in table 3.11 are based on the assumption that the relevant alternative to the NGPA was deregulation (that is, in the supply-and-demand model, the regulatory variable for 1979–1989 is assumed to have a value of zero). Both regulated and deregulated prices should have been high in this period due to low-levels of additions to reserves and production. NGPA prices were 80 cents per mcf lower than deregulated prices would have been in 1978–1979 (table 3.11, fig. 3.6). But NGPA prices would have more than caught up to these prices for unregulated market conditions; indeed, NGPA-regulated prices increased by 57 cents per mcf in 1981–1982. NGPA prices leveled off at $2.32 per mmBtu in 1982, whereas unregulated prices would have been at $1.29 per mmBtu in 1982 (fig. 3.6).

The gains to producers from prices too high were substantial, but these gains

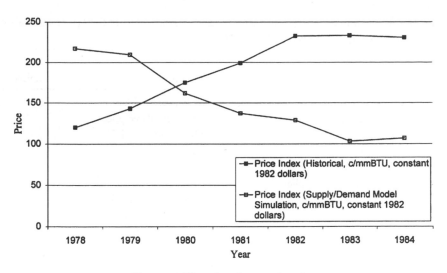

Figure 3.6. The price of gas, 1978–1984

Table 3.11. Historical and model simulation prices, quantities, and reserves, as affected by field price regulation, following passage of the NGPA, 1978–1984

Year	Production (historical, tcf)	Production (supply-demand model simulation, tcf)	Reserves (historical, tcf)	Reserves (supply-demand model simulation, tcf)	Price index (historical, c/mmBtu, constant 1982 dollars)	Price index (supply-demand model simulation, c/mmBtu constant 1982 dollars)
1978	18.90	18.84	182.31	194.29	120.14	217.09
1979	19.42	19.12	180.83	210.96	143.20	209.56
1980	19.19	19.85	172.99	227.80	175.10	161.99
1981	18.94	20.78	170.67	240.86	199.35	137.50
1982	17.55	21.04	173.71	246.84	232.78	129.04
1983	15.82	20.95	171.14	245.76	233.41	103.57
1984	17.14	21.98	171.17	247.27	230.77	107.13

Sources: DOE/EIA historical statistics; DOE/EIA 1996; model simulations that establish equilibrium unregulated price index and quantity, as explained in the text.

Notes: [1]In chained 1982 cents, calculated using GDP implicit price deflators.

[2]Converted from c/mcf to c/mmBtu using dry production heat content.

[3]Represents price of gas sold and delivered by local distribution companies and does not reflect gas transported for the others.

[4]Reserves are at beginning of year.

Table 3.12. Gains and losses of producers and customers from field price regulation, following passage of the NGPA, 1978–1984

	Method of estimation	Estimated 1982 dollars (in millions)
Losses of consumers from WACOG prices higher than market clearing prices.	Difference between market clearing and regulated prices multiplied by historical production. (Area *A*)	44,531
Gains of producers from supplies at WACOG prices above market clearing prices.	Difference between market clearing and regulated prices multiplied by historical production. (Area *A*)	44,531
Gains of consumers from lower prices due to sell-off of excess gas in the spot market.	Difference between regulated and market clearing price times difference between regulated and market clearing production divided by two. (Area *B*)	40,698
Losses of producers because of sell-off at spot prices below WACOG prices levels.	Difference between spot and supply price on that part of historical production sold at spot. (Area *C*)	89,604

Source: As explained in the text and derived from supply-demand model simulations.
Note: Aggregated, but not discounted, over the years 1978–1984.

were more than canceled by losses from the low prices they received from the surplus that followed. Gains to producers exceeded $44 billion, but losses from having to dump the "bubble" into spot markets were greater than $89 billion (table 3.12). The losses to consumers from the high NGPA prices were $44 billion, whereas their gains in the spot market were $40 billion. These results for consumers and producers, then, indicate that both lost from $4 billion to $45 billion over the seven-year period of NGPA implementation.

If there had been complete price decontrol, reserves would have increased to levels 40 to 50 tcf greater than actual levels by 1984. Production as a consequence would have been 3 to 5 tcf higher each year (see fig. 3.7: additions to reserves exceed production under simulated "no regulated" conditions). Deregulation would have caused sharp price increases in the late 1970s, which would

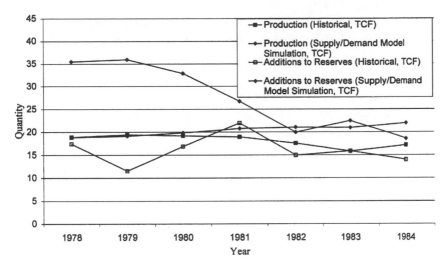

Figure 3.7. Production and additions to reserves, 1978–1984

have increased reserves and production, so that by the early 1980s the market would have cleared at price levels below NGPA-regulated price levels. Additional reserves, generated by deregulation, would have taken production to higher levels that would have then resulted in lower long-run prices.

CONCLUSION

Two sustained periods of disruption mark the 1970s and 1980s gas field markets. The first took the form of substantial supply shortages, with consequent shutdowns of commercial and industrial user facilities in the mid-1970s. The second consisted of equally substantial gas surpluses, with reduced take by pipeline purchasers operating under reserve contracts signed at excessive, partially regulated prices in the early 1980s. Both of these disequilibrium conditions can be associated with policies of the federal regulatory commissions (FPC and then FERC), first while seeking to provide gas at low, fixed prices over long periods of time and second to solve shortages developed by the first without raising prices to consumers.

The nature of service, by contract prescribed by regulation, determined these results. From the inception of regulation, the Federal Power Commission required that service take place under long-term contracts for dedicated reserves, in which production from reserves was determined by pipeline buyers and price was indexed on new contract prices. By holding new contract prices down, the commission determined that prices would be fixed in line with those given by market conditions five to ten years earlier.

The commission-determined price trend held until 1974. Then price increases exceeded 20 percent per annum, and continued at that rate each year until 1977, by which time the price was twice the 1974 level. Even so, market-clearing prices that would sustain production required to meet demands were still 15 percent higher than actual prices (see table 3.1). If market-clearing prices had been realized in the 1960s, supplies of reserves would have been 10 to 15 percent greater, and demands would have been reduced by 5 to 10 percent.

By the mid-1970s the regulated gas prices caused shortages that exceeded levels never previously realized in energy markets. Shortages resulted in consumers incurring losses in excess of $13 billion; producers lost in excess of $44 billion (see table 3.2).

The subsequent experiment in phased decontrol of wellhead prices sought to increase supplies while not increasing prices to consumers for gas from these reserve contracts. The implementation of the NGPA resulted in contracts for deep offshore gas, and for such out-of-market high cost supplies as coalseam gas, at prices far above competitive levels. It shifted gas from intrastate to interstate consumers where the shortage was the greatest. As old contracts expired and new contracts phased in, the index price doubled. Demands declined by 20 percent over the first few years of the 1980s. Resulting excess supply under long-term contracts caused widespread pipeline refusals to take.

Again, there were no gains for affected producers or consumers. At prices 20 to 70 percent too high, gains for some producers were large. The dollar value of what they sold on contract over what they would have realized under deregulation probably exceeded $44 billion. But they lost on sales that had to be diverted into the spot market at below-competitive spot prices by an amount that exceeded $89 billion. Losses of customers from prices that were too high exceeded $44 billion, $4 billion more than what they gained from low-priced spot market purchases. Altogether, both producers and consumers lost from the so-called deregulatory process in the first years under the NGPA (see table 3.12).

These, in general, were the effects of regulation in the 1970s and 1980s on the performance of the gas industry. Policies put in place to control prices did not make consumers better off, whether they were designed to raise price or lower price. Nor did they improve the lot of producers, even when raising price above market clearing levels. But at the end of this period further deregulation offered an opportunity for better performance. Excess supplies generated by the NGPA became the source for the development of a new market system in spot direct sales of gas at the wellhead to final retailers, brokers, and dealers. This market, a dumping ground for excess production from failed contracts with the pipelines, led to the development of new markets for unbundled gas and transportation in the 1990s. Regulation and deregulation in these markets, and their effect on industry performance, are the subject of the next chapter.

Chapter 4 The Partial Deregulation of Transportation and the Creation of a Single North American Gas Market

Out of the morass of the 1980s wellhead price regulation there emerged a new network of product and transport markets, some regulated and others partially deregulated. The regulatory solutions to the gas shortages of the 1970s, which led to excess supply through the mid-1980s, made the case for restructuring wellhead and city gate merchant contracts. The emergence of spot markets for gas outside regulation made it possible for gas users to obtain production separate from transportation. FERC and the courts responded by easing access to separate transportation service for producers, dealers, distributors, and industrial consumers.

In Orders 436 and 636, FERC first offered the option and then required the replacement of pipeline merchant service with common-carrier delivery of gas owned by others. Unbundled gas production and transportation at the city gate led to the elimination of long-term contract sales by producers to pipeline buyers at the wellhead. Spot markets were established to put excess production from the "bubble" into the transmission system and were followed by the creation of financial instruments in gas futures. Spot purchases hedged by futures became an alternative to long-term contracts for managing risks in product availability. Access to product and to contract transportation separately made it possible to substitute flexible combinations of services for pipeline merchant contracts in assuring supplies for consumers.

Individual pipelines began switching gas at "market hubs," locations where they overlapped with other carriers. Hub markets developed in spot and contract gas, and also in firm and interruptible transport services. With open entry in these new markets and many additional sources of supply, these markets became more competitive; even so, federal regulation did not disappear as the controlling factor in the performance of transporters.

But at this point in time, to make regulation more "light handed," the commission replaced its system of cost-of-service rates in merchant contracts with a "three-option" approach. Shippers and pipelines could choose traditional rate controls based on "cost of service," or they could negotiate their own rates, or, third, the commission would set "market-based" capped rates and adjust these rates downward for increased productivity over time. These options applied to firm transportation in both the primary (pipeline) and secondary (resale) markets while interruptible transportation was decontrolled.

SPOT GAS AND UNBUNDLED
TRANSPORTATION MARKETS

The full-scale development of spot markets for natural gas presaged regulatory requirements for unbundling transportation from ownership of the product. The first step toward unbundling was taken in the late 1970s, with FERC Order 27, which allowed certain consumers such as schools and hospitals to enter into gas ownership contracts with producers and also authorized interstate pipelines to transport this gas. In 1985, FERC Order 436 extended this option to contract for independent transportation to all pipeline shippers.[1] The order required pipelines to offer to unbundle service so that any gas owner (field producer, broker, or local retail distribution company) could choose among pipeline providers of transportation services to carry gas it independently purchased in Texas or Louisiana. The transportation service was to be on the same terms as bundled merchant service by a pipeline that owned gas, given that the order sought nondiscriminatory access for independent owner-shippers.

By 1990 the major pipelines had begun to provide transport service only for gas suppliers. But FERC Order 500 in 1987 went the next-to-last step toward removing pipelines from gas wellhead markets by requiring "open-access" transportation for gas at the wellhead owned by others. This required a new FERC process to cash the pipelines out from existing gas contracts, which moved to eliminate the highest-priced contracts. FERC continued to require bundled service to retailers that demanded "on-call" deliveries on peak heating days at the same time, however.

In this period, price controls at the wellhead were finally phased out completely. The long process that began in the Natural Gas Policy Act of 1978 was extended in FERC Orders 519 and 523, which raised all the price ceilings on old gas. A congressional initiative in the Wellhead Price Decontrol Act provided statutory authority for complete decontrol of wellhead prices in 1993.[2] With the Order 500 buyout of old contracts, prices in markets for contract and those for spot gas began to move together.

FERC went the last step, to establish open access to separate transportation, in Order 436, which allowed a pipeline to build new facilities under an "optional expedited certificate," taking years off the approval process, and allowed pipelines to charge negotiated rates for space in new lines. Blanket certificate rights to build "eligible facilities" in incumbent pipelines were also issued, thus facilitating development of overlaps at major gas transfer locations (hubs).[3] By the beginning of the 1990s, the major pipelines offered firm service under contracts in tariffs for transportation of gas owned by other suppliers. The tariffs were based on straight fixed variable (SFV) rates, consisting of a monthly charge to recover depreciation and equity returns and usage charges to recover variable costs on each mcf of gas delivered. In contracts for firm capacity, the monthly charges were regulated, based on cost of service, determined by commission review procedures in place since implementation of the NGA. Pipelines and shippers could negotiate prices lower than SFV firm capacity rates to be put in place without review by FERC. These prices had to be "responsible" for fixed costs equivalent to those recovered in SFV rates whether charged or not. Both SFV and negotiated rates applied to committed pipeline capacity; but a shipper could, after contracting for firm capacity, offer that space in the "release" or resale market. The prices in this secondary market could not exceed the FERC limit on SFV firm capacity rate.

The thrust of restructuring and market creation was to establish transportation-only services to any city gate and industrial consumer at market prices. Transportation was to become a separate competitive market. Even so, firm transportation was still price regulated in the cost-of-service–based process. Negotiated transportation contract prices could be lower, and not determined by the commission, as long as the shipper had as a ceiling price recourse to a regulated firm rate. A shipper could complain to FERC that it was being "unduly discriminated against or [was] worse off, or [was] being offered a lower rate but lack of access to capacity."[4] SFV rates applied on firm transportation; they then were discounted in negotiated prices. By the winter of 1996–1997, firm contracts accounted for more than 80 percent of capacity, but 20 percent of that had been released and used by other shippers under secondary transactions.[5] The remaining 20 percent of original capacity that was uncommitted was offered as interruptible transportation (IT) at discount prices.

In 1992, FERC Order 636 completed this last step in restructuring the transportation level of the industry. This order made firm transportation subject to regulated price caps rather than cost of service and set out conditions for prices on "released" transportation. Market developments and this order caused industry performance to be subject to more of the rigors of competition, but with rate regulation of transporters still in effect.

FERC ORDER 636 AS PARTIAL DEREGULATION

In the last months of the Bush administration, the Federal Energy Regulatory Commission put in place Order 636 to specify that the natural gas industry be required to restructure itself into separate production, transmission, and distribution service industries.[6] The interstate pipelines had to divest their contracts to purchase gas at the wellhead and become carriers only of supplies owned by others. Justifications for this requirement were provided, to the effect that pro-competitive gains to consumers would result from reduced prices at the city gate as pipeline gas contracts at high prices were eliminated and replaced by spot gas at low prices.

The effects of requiring separation of pipeline services were significant and widespread. The experience from gas deliveries between fifteen city-pairs over the period 1989–1994 is indicative; transport prices did become more competitive, at levels below FERC firm tariff rates between hub centers and major points of delivery. Regulatory price caps on contracts for firm pipeline capacity became redundant except for short periods when there was peak-period tightness of capacity available for commitment to shippers.

Order 636. The commission in July 1991 issued a notice of proposed rulemaking known as the "Mega-NOPR" to specify a plan for mandatory unbundling of gas and transportation.[7] The outcome of public review of the

Mega-NOPR and commission deliberation was FERC Orders 636, 636-A, and 636-B. These orders required numerous changes in industry structure and practices, four of which potentially affected gas industry performance.

First, pipelines were required to provide unbundled firm and interruptible transportation service to other owners of gas supplies. Pipeline gas-plus-transportation services had to be converted to transportation only. The pipelines had to provide equal access for all shippers to firm and interruptible capacity. Second, transportation had to exclude storage that was to be provided on an open-access basis by other sources. Third, firm transportation services were to be priced according to the straight fixed variable method, with capital costs recovered in a monthly demand charge for service and variable costs recovered in a per mcf delivery charge. The fourth major requirement was the method by which unused capacity would be marketed; pipelines were to develop "release" programs by which they or their shippers could offer unused capacity in spot markets posted on electronic bulletin boards (EBBs).

These four requirements gave gas buyers the option of firm or interruptible pipeline transportation capacity to move gas from field or downstream points to city gate or wholesale markets for resale or use. Interruptible and released capacity in a secondary market would provide alternatives to firm space. Further, shippers could substitute released and interruptible transport in combinations they put together with storage to provide a secure service to compete with pipeline firm service.

FERC expected that this would "improve the competitive structure of the natural gas industry and at the same time maintain an adequate and reliable service."[8] The commission intended to accomplish this "in a way that continues to ensure consumers access to an adequate supply of gas at a reasonable price."[9] With more buyers at the wellhead and more sources of transport capacity, including released capacity at critical access locations, then more gas would arrive at the city gate at lower prices. Thus Orders 636, 636-A, and 636-B made gas prices and transportation rates responsive to supply and demand conditions in an emerging national market for various services.

Even so, FERC continued to regulate tariff rates on firm transportation. Pipelines still had the opportunity to recover all costs but no more under SFV price ceilings. Even on interruptible services with direct alternatives in secondary markets, any volumetric price had to be capped by the firm tariff rate calculated on the basis of a 100 percent pipeline load factor.

The market effects of restructured transportation. The development of switching of gas supplies at intersection points of the individual pipelines had the effect of putting in place a single network connecting all the major producing basins with city gates throughout the United States and western Canada. That one market was the proximate result can be shown by the degree of integration of the individual pipelines into a single network. The test of whether the network is fully integrated, with all nodes connected and with positive transportation costs between each pair of nodes, is whether prices for wellhead and city gate gas at different locations follow "the law of one price," so that the difference at two locations is equal to the transportation charge from the upstream location to the downstream location. Observations of prices for gas at sixty-three nodes from 1986 to 1997 indicate that 82 percent of pairs of nodes in fact have gas prices that follow the law of one price. Even though the physical network does not have connections between all nodes, arbitrage unites them in one network, substituting nonexistent routes with existing parts of the network.

After FERC Order 636, transportation costs to gas buyers declined each year between major market hubs, as estimated by the difference between commodity prices at these nodes. Consumers saved almost $200 million per year in gas transportation charges on deliveries to nine major city gates alone. The total decline in transportation charges between 1986 and 1997, based on extrapolation of these nine city results, can be estimated at $2.18 billion.

Have transportation service prices become more competitive in these new integrated markets for transportation? The answer is also an empirical matter. We estimate, once again, the market price of transportation services by the difference between the receipt and delivered prices of spot gas at any city-pair. The transportation price per mcf of gas, for example, between Illinois and Louisiana equals the difference between spot gas prices for sale at those two locations. If it were greater than this difference, then none would be shipped; if it were less, then brokers would ship more until the downstream price fell and/or the upstream price rose to cause the excess to disappear. Given this equilibrating process, which determines transport price behavior in hub markets, then gas price differences can be compared to regulated tariff transport rates to determine the extent to which a competitive market has developed that has bypassed the regulatory process. If there is limited competition, then individual pipelines providing service and setting individual transport prices between a city-pair have an effect on the spot gas price difference between that city-pair. If competition is effective, however, then gas price differences between city-pairs of the same distance do not vary with the number of pipelines between these city-pairs. Competitive sources of service characteristically set prices that converge as long as the largest sources cannot control aggregate pipeline capacity.[10] The alternative hypothesis is that regulated prices or discount prices in regulated markets still tend to fall as the number of comparable-sized pipelines offering service capacity increases.[11]

Estimating the price difference in spot gas prices at receipt and delivery locations in a city-pair yields:

Transactions Transport Price = $(P_d - P_u) = f(D, HHI, TARIFF)$

where:

P_d = spot gas price at the downstream city gate;

P_u = spot gas price at the upstream field or delivery point (market hub);

D = distance between the upstream market center and the downstream city gate;

HHI = Herfindahl-Hirschman transport concentration index, equal to the sum of the squares of pipeline market capacity shares for delivery at that location; and

$TARIFF$ = tariff projected firm capacity charge, cents per mcf, at full capacity.

Gas prices at selected city gates and market hubs were obtained from *Natural Gas Week* and *Natural Gas Intelligence;* these trade journals report spot prices at selected locations for three consecutive weeks and the change at the close of "bid week." Transportation distances between upstream market hubs and downstream city gates were compiled from *Pennwell Books'* maps of natural gas pipelines of the United States and Canada.[12] The Herfindahl Index for each city gate was estimated from peak day deliveries as reported in annual *FERC Form 2 Reports* of the individual pipelines.[13] City gate and hubs used to test the relationship are listed in table 4.1. The downstream city gates (several of which are also market hubs) are Boston; Chicago; Detroit; Lebanon, Ohio; New York City; Tuscola, Illinois; and the California-Arizona border location at Topock, Arizona. The upstream hubs are Erath, Louisiana; Guymon, Oklahoma; Katy, Texas; Monroe, Louisiana; and Waha, Texas. The city-pairs for which price differences were estimated are all downstream city gate and upstream market centers on the same row in the table.[14]

Average city-pair price differences as estimates of transactions transport prices were less than tariff rates during the period January 1989 to April 1994 for every city-pair except Waha to Topock (see table 4.2). In an attempt to explain variations in these prices, a Box-Cox model has been fitted as follows:

$$(P_d - P_u)^{\lambda t} = b_1 + b_2 (P_d - P_{u\lambda t-1}) + b_3 D^\lambda + b_4 HHI^\lambda + b_5 TARIFF^\lambda$$
$$+ b_6 WINTER^\lambda + \epsilon^{15}$$

The left-hand side of this equation is the transport price with P_d as the gas spot price at destination and Pu as the gas spot price at origin. The right-hand side includes the same variable lagged one period, based on assuming that the equilibrium price difference is achieved only after multiple periods. The second explanatory variable, distance D, should have a positive coefficient, given that costs increase with distance. The third explanatory variable, *WINTER*, tests the hypothesis that there is less competition in the peak heating season.[16] The *TARIFF* variable tests the hypothesis that prices for transportation over the period of unbundling were determined by rate limits imposed by FERC on firm transportation. The last explanatory variable, *HHI*, would have a positive coefficient only if the number of pipelines affects the level of transport price in a noncompetitive process.

To test these hypotheses, 512 observations of gas spot price differences between fifteen city-pairs over the period January 1989 to April 1994 were used to estimate the Box-Cox equation (table 4.3). The statistically significant determinants of the transactions transport price are lagged prices for the same city-pair and the city-pair distance.[17] The elasticities of the transport price with respect to these variables have been estimated as shown; the significant elasticities are

Table 4.1. City-pairs for establishing transportation "transactions" prices

Market center		City gate
Erath, La.		Chicago
Erath, La.		New York City
Guymon, Okla.		Detroit
Katy, Tex.		Chicago
Katy, Tex.		New York City
Katy, Tex.	via Lebanon, Ohio	New York City
Monroe, La.		Chicago
Monroe, La.		Detroit
Monroe, La.		New York City
Monroe, La.	via Lebanon, Ohio	New York City
Waha, Tex.		Topock, Ariz.

Source: As explained in the text.

Table 4.2. Average city-pair price differentials and tariff transport rates, January 1989–April 1994 ($/mmBtu)

Origin	Destination	Destination city gate HHI	Price differences[1]	Tariff transportation rates[2]
Erath, La.	Chicago	3200	0.18	0.27
Erath, La.	New York City	2900	0.44	0.48
Monroe, La.	Chicago	3200	0.15	0.43
Monroe, La.	Detroit	4100	0.28	0.97
Monroe, La.	New York City	2900	0.41	0.62
Monroe, La.	New York City (Lebanon, Ohio)	2700	0.44	0.68
New York City	Boston	6100	0.21	0.21
Guymon, Okla.	Tuscola, Ill.	3100	0.22	0.45
Guymon, Okla.	Chicago	3200	0.33	0.36
Guymon, Okla.	Detroit	4100	0.48	0.51
Katy, Tex.	Chicago	3200	0.21	0.25
Katy, Tex.	New York City	2900	0.48	0.51
Katy, Tex.	New York City (Lebanon, Ohio)	2700	0.50	0.87
Opal, Wyo.	Topock, Ariz.	3900	0.60	0.74
Waha, Tex.	Topock, Ariz.	3900	0.46	0.34

Source: As explained in the text.
Notes: [1] Price difference equal the difference in delivered spot prices between the city-pairs.
[2] Transport rate is the maximum interruptible transportation tariff on the pipeline(s) connected to the city-pairs.

those for lagged price differences (0.537) and for transport distance (0.171). Also the coefficient of *TARIFF* indicates that tariff rate changes were reflected in transport prices between city-pairs; that is, the elasticity of *TARIFF* evaluated at its mean equals 0.171, indicating that a 10 percent increase in the tariff rate increased actual transport prices by 1.7 percent.

There is no indication that any hypothetical pipeline market power determined transport prices. The coefficient of *HHI,* though positive, is not statistically significant, failing to reject the hypothesis of no price level concentration relationship. The coefficient of *WINTER* did not differ from zero, so that the hypothesis that there was price leveraging in the peak heating season also can be rejected. In all, tariff rates applied to a small percentage of annual throughput, and as pipelines matched offers of other lines or bids for use of released capac-

Table 4.3. Regression equation for city· pair gas
price differences

Independent variable	Parameter estimate	Box-Cox elasticity at means
Intercept	−0.48343	—
	(−2.687)	
$(P_d - P_u)_{t-1}$	0.53386	0.537
	(14.416)	
Distance	0.09390	0.171
	(2.782)	
HHI	0.25820	0.258
	(1.058)	
Tariff	0.13969	0.171
	(2.783)	
Winter	0.01342	0.017
	(1.111)	
λ	0.43906	—
	(11.671)	

Source: As explained in the text.
Notes: t-statistics for H_0: b = 0 are in parentheses.
Dependent variable = $(P_d - P_u)_t$.
Adjusted R-squared = 0.43.

ity of their own customers, then transportation prices were no longer determined by regulated rate schedules.

There is an additional question as to whether the extent of discounting of
prices for transportation depended on specific pipeline locational power. This
can be indicated by defining the discount, $DISC_t$, as equal to the tariff rate
(*TARIFF*) minus the city-pair price difference $(P_u - P_d)$ for each city-pair in
the sample. If pipelines were less able to set rates as numbers of pipelines increased at some location, then the discount $DISC_t$ would depend on its previous level and on the *HHI* relevant to that (city-pair) location,

$$DISC_t = b_1 [DISC_{t-1}] + b_2 [HHI]$$

with $b_1 > 0$, and $b_2 < 0$. And if the determinant were location specific, so that
a particular pipeline counted in setting prices, then the dummy variable for
pipelines would be significant. Two equations to test these hypotheses are
shown in table 4.4.

Table 4.4. Regression equation for price discounts

Independent variable	Parameter estimate	
	Model One	Model Two
Intercept	−0.064	−0.031
	(−1.023)	(−1.811)
DISC$_{t-1}$	0.743	0.552
	(25.808)	(16.790)
HHI	0.304	—
	(1.525)	
ANR	—	0.300
		(7.936)
Panhandle	—	0.138
		(3.910)
NGPL	—	0.090
		(2.710)
Texas Eastern	—	0.108
		(4.526)
El Paso	—	0.024
		(−0.807)
Transwestern	—	−0.008
		(−0.270)
Kern River	—	0.166
		(4.117)
Adjusted *R*-squared	0.5718	0.6179

Source: As explained in the text.
Notes: *t*-statistics for H$_0$: b = 0 are in parentheses.
Dependent variable = DISC$_t$.

In the first equation, the coefficient of the lagged dependent variable is pos-itive (0.773) and has a t-statistic that is significant but that for *HHI,* while also positive, is not statistically significant. The second equation points up a pattern of discounting that occurs not in city-pairs but in regions of the country. The three Midwest pipelines (ANR Pipeline, Panhandle, and Natural Gas Pipeline) had significantly larger discounts than pipelines to the East (Transco, as the "base" pipeline, and Texas Eastern) or to the West Coast (El Paso and Tran-swestern; but Kern River, a later entrant, had a significant and larger discount).

There is a variant on this test to find the influence of pipeline concentration on competition in transportation markets. In the case of few pipelines, the price difference for natural gas at the two hubs is a function of the marginal cost of transportation, the elasticity of demand, pipeline concentration, and conjectural variation—that is, "the toughness of competition" in the market. The objective of the test is to compare the degree of competition in the transportation market before and after FERC Orders 636, 636-A, and 636-B were issued in 1991, as measured by the average conjectural variation in the market. For a data set on node spot gas prices for 1990 to 1997, for twenty-two origin and nine destination nodes, the coefficient on *HHI* turned out to be 0.215. Marginal cost is parameterized as a sum of quadratic function of distance between the gas origin and destination and the price of gas at origin. Assuming an elasticity of gas demand of -0.7, we arrive at a conjectural variation u of -0.85. For comparison, Cournot (noncooperative price setting) corresponds to $u = 0$, while Bertrand (fully competitive price setting) equals $u = -1$. This results implies that the degree of competition is severe, even though each region has only three or four equal-sized carriers. We reach the conclusion that it is not the number of carriers but the number of participants in secondary transportation markets for excess spot and contract space that defines competition. Allowing for time variation in the coefficient on concentration and again assuming the elasticity of demand of -0.7, the estimate for u equals -0.65 for the year 1990 and -0.89 for the period 1994–1997. This implies that Order 636 had a positive effect on transport competition, most likely by inducing entry by independent marketers offering space in the secondary market for transportation.

Thus, there were four critical changes to pipeline rate behavior in these transition years from merchant to unbundled services. First, actual prices for transport-only services in these years were below FERC regulated tariff rates. Second, changes in FERC tariff rates had limited effects on changes in actual transport prices: for a 10 percent tariff reduction, prices went down by less than 2 percent. Third, the size of discounts on tariff rates did not depend on supplier concentration at various city gates, but deeper discounts were found at hubs in the Midwest. Fourth, peak-season transport prices were not significantly higher, implying that market power was not there for pipelines to squeeze out higher prices for transportation during peak heating periods. These four changes support the conclusion that market, not regulatory conditions, determined prices for transportation service in the early to middle 1990s. Regulatory controls of so-called noncompetitive transportation market rates were not determinants of actual terms and conditions for market transportation.

The role of capacity release. During the 1993–1994 winter heating season, markets in released pipeline capacity developed rapidly. Supply consisted of firm capacity in a pipeline, as provided by a shipper with a capacity contract but not using that capacity. Demand consisted of purchases of such contracts by other shippers with access to substitute firm or interruptible contracts on that pipeline. The prices in these secondary sales in the first half of the 1990s departed widely from regulated rates on firm transport. For example, in the spring of 1994 in California, where there were three independent pipelines (El Paso, Transwestern, and Kern River), the major shippers, Southern California Gas Co. (SoCal Gas) and Pacific Gas and Electric (PG&E) offered release capacity at 75 percent of the average firm capacity tariff rate and then at 30 percent of the tariff rate in August. Discounting increased when SoCal and PG&E began to offer "volumetric" prices for released capacity, under which an acquiring shipper was responsible for paying a portion of the demand charge. (For example, if a buyer of release capacity acquired 10,000 mcf/day of firm capacity under a 20 percent volumetric offer, the seller would pay the demand charge on only 8,000 mcf/day).

El Paso completed more than six hundred transactions in release capacity by April 1994 and a larger number of transactions in the next two months, with total volumes increasing from 0.772 bcf on March 8 to 1.062 bcf on April 8, 1994; more than 50 percent of its throughput was carried at discounts of 20 percent on the tariff rate, and 40 percent was carried at discounts of 55 percent or more. Subsequently both PG&E and SoCal had release capacity at discounts of 60 to 75 percent of tariff (although they paid full tariff rates to the pipelines under their long-term contracts). Pacific Gas Transmission also transported secondary capacity volumes at discounts that averaged 50 to 60 percent of the tariff firm capacity rate.

Given that the winter 1993–1994 market for gas supplies into the Midwest and East was subject to severe weather, there were very few releases of firm capacity at that time. But spring and summer were marked by abundant release capacity, with marketers of spot gas seeking short-term transportation at deep discounts on tariff rates. By early 1995, the Interstate Natural Gas Association of America (INGAA) reported that the majority of release capacity was acquired at prices well below the maximum allowed rates,[18] that is, that release capacity awarded through an open-bid process had prices that on average were 22 percent of the tariff rate.

A second analysis of competitiveness. The introduction of open-access transformed transportation into partially competitive and partially regulated markets. How competitive the result has been can be indicated by the profit performance of the pipelines. The annual returns to equity for thirty-three of the largest pipelines, for 1991–1996, vary with line capacity, the rate of capacity utilization, and regional market share. If markets have been noncompetitive, then profit is greater from market advantages when the pipeline is larger and when capacity utilization is greater. Profits vary with market share in markets marked by noncompetitive price formation. But if markets are fully competitive, only the overall industry return determines a pipeline's return on equity.

Total pipeline capacity is measured in mcf/day of interstate gas flow, as the sum of capacities on individual interstate branches. Capacity utilization is defined as the ratio of the average actual gas flow to maximum flow capacity. Market share is calculated on the presumption that states are relevant pipeline markets and that share is defined as the ratio of individual pipeline gas flow to the total gas flow in that state. If the pipeline delivers gas to five states, then that pipeline market share is the arithmetic average of the five state shares.

If we list the largest ten pipelines in descending order by total interstate capacity, we see clearly that there is no straightforward relationship between firm capacity, utilization, and share (table 4.5). As total firm capacity monotonically declines from more than 31 mmcf/day for the largest company, Transcontinental, to 10 mmcf/day for the tenth largest, Texas Gas Transmission, capacity utilization first declines, to 39 percent, for the sixth largest firm, El Paso, and to 37 percent for the eighth, Northern Natural, but increases to 75 percent for the tenth largest company, Texas Gas Transmission. Pipeline share also does not exhibit any clear relation to pipeline size: share is largest for the ninth largest firm, Northern Border, at 0.55, but is at low levels for most other firms, in a range be-

Table 4.5. The largest ten pipelines by estimated capacity

	Total firm capacity	Capacity utilization	Share	Average return on equity
Transcontinental	**31,471**	0.70885	0.20258	6.7143
Tenneco	**26,741**	0.71061	0.07806	5.2143
ANR	**24,939**	0.53022	0.07432	16.6714
Texas Eastern	**24,907**	0.70320	0.10091	7.9143
NGPL	**16,946**	0.57422	0.07554	16.5714
El Paso	**13,503**	0.39612	0.12217	10.6714
Trunkline	**12,710**	0.59665	0.09427	6.4857
Northern Natural	**12,240**	0.37274	0.06387	20.2429
Northern Border	**12,024**	0.66119	0.55209	19.1143
Texas Gas Transmission	**10,489**	0.75595	0.03742	10.7143

Sources: FERC Form 2 (1983–1996) for return on equity; FERC Form 567 for all volume shipments and capacity.

Table 4.6. The ten pipelines with the highest rates of capacity utilization

	Total firm capacity	Capacity utilization	Share	Average return on equity
Iroquois	1,633	0.92115	0.13781	10.525
Kern River	2,331	0.91076	0.32618	13.800
Pacific Gas Transmission	9,792	0.88826	0.52071	8.9428
Great Lakes	8,939	0.84032	0.37427	14.086
Trailblazer	2,420	0.81958	0.15114	11.871
Viking	981	0.78300	0.04509	11.714
Texas Gas Transmission	10,489	0.75595	0.03742	10.714
Florida Gas Transmission	4,470	0.73249	0.26292	13.271
Tenneco	26,741	0.71061	0.07806	5.2143
Transcontinental	31,471	0.70885	0.20258	6.7143

Source: See table 4.5.

tween 0.07 and 0.12. The determined variable, average return on equity, is low for the largest firms (6.7 percent per year for Transcontinental and 5.2 percent for Tenneco) but is as high as 20.2 percent per year for the eighth largest company, Northern Border.

If we measure the largest ten pipelines in terms of capacity utilization (table 4.6), only three pipelines match those listed in table 4.5. The largest capacity firms, Transcontinental and Tenneco, are at the bottom of the list of top-capacity utilization firms. The smaller companies have higher capacity utilization than medium- and large-sized firms. A recent entrant, Iroquois, which started operations in 1993, had the highest capacity utilization, 92 percent, and as utilization declines, market share first increases and then declines. No clear relation is indicated between capacity utilization and return on equity, which ranges between 5 percent and 14 percent per year, with 14 percent for the second and fourth firms and 13 percent for the eighth firm but only 10 percent for the top-ranked firm.

The ten firms with the largest market shares in gas transported are listed in table 4.7. The shares decline from 0.55 for Northern Border to 0.14 for Iroquois. Total capacity declines with share, with one exception, the largest capacity firm but seventh in market share. All companies in this sample demonstrate quite significant capacity utilization, with a minimum at 54 percent for Algonquin and maximum for Iroquois at 92 percent, the tenth firm ranked by state share. Yet the determined variable, return on equity, essentially follows a random walk, high for the largest share firm, lowest for the second largest share

Table 4.7. The ten pipelines with the largest market shares

	Total firm capacity	Capacity utilization	Share	Average return on equity
Northern Border	12,024	0.66119	**0.55209**	19.114
Pacific Gas Transmission	9,792	0.88826	**0.52071**	8.9429
Great Lakes	8,939	0.84032	**0.37427**	14.085
Algonquin	3,790	0.54032	**0.32878**	14.943
Kern River	2,331	0.91076	**0.32618**	13.800
Florida Gas Transmission	4,470	0.73249	**0.26292**	13.271
Transcontinental	31,471	0.70885	**0.20258**	6.714
Wyoming Interstate	743	0.70671	**0.15769**	8.457
Trailblazer	2,420	0.81958	**0.15114**	11.871
Iroquois	1,633	0.92115	**0.13781**	10.525

Source: See table 4.5.

firm, then higher for the third- and fourth-ranked companies. No clear relation between profit return and capacity utilization can been seen here.

Returns on equity for the ten most profitable pipelines are given in table 4.8. The highest return pipelines should have the largest capacity, the highest rates of utilization, and the largest market shares. But the company with the highest return line is medium-sized, Northern Natural, with a low-capacity utilization of 37 percent and a small average market share of 6 percent. The second

Table 4.8. The ten pipelines with the highest return on equity

	Total firm capacity	Capacity utilization	Share	Average return on equity
Northern Natural	12,240	0.37274	0.06387	**20.243**
Northern Border	12,024	0.66119	0.55209	**19.114**
Colorado Interstate	2,524	0.49330	0.04139	**17.229**
ANR	24,939	0.53022	0.07432	**16.671**
NGPL	16,946	0.57422	0.07554	**16.571**
Algonquin	3,790	0.54032	0.32878	**14.943**
Northwest Pipeline	7,912	0.28945	0.09035	**14.443**
Great Lakes	8,939	0.84032	0.37427	**14.086**
Transwestern	5,236	0.27098	0.05878	**14.086**
Kern River	2,331	0.91076	0.32618	**13.800**

Source: See table 4.5.

highest return pipeline is Northern Border, again medium-sized with medium-capacity utilization, but with the largest average market share of 55 percent. Further in this ranking, as return on equity declines, the other variables experience changes without any obvious pattern. Total capacity varies from a low of 2,331 mcf/day for the tenth highest, Kern River, to a high of 24,939 mcf/day for the fourth highest, ANR Pipeline. Capacity utilization is in the low range of 27–55 percent, with exceptions at 84 percent for the eighth-ranked company, Great Lakes, and 91 percent for the tenth-ranked firm, Kern River. Shares increase and then decrease as average return on equity declines.

To determine the effects of each of these variables together on the return on equity, a regression equation was constructed (table 4.9). The lagged (previous year) values of return on equity (ROE) explain 20.6 percent of the variance in current year ROE. (The coefficient for the lagged value is statistically significant.) Firm capacity has a negative effect on ROE (the coefficient is insignificant). Capacity utilization also has a negative effect on ROE (the coefficient is insignificant). Market share has a positive effect on ROE (the coefficient, too, is not statistically significant), implying that firms with even limited market power have not been able to generate higher returns on equity.

In conclusion, there is no systematic pattern of association between size or share or capacity utilization and return on equity for the interstate pipelines in the years immediately following the unbundling of gas and transportation. If

Table 4.9. Return on pipeline equity as determined by structural variables

Variable	Estimates of coefficients
Constant	89.542
	(7.691)
Lagged return on equity	0.206
	(0.066)
Total firm capacity$*10^{-3}$	0.040
	(0.055)
Capacity utilization	−1.967
	(2.358)
Market share	5.157
	(3.597)
Adjusted R-squared (N = 186)	0.057

Source: Data from tables 4.5–4.9; standard errors of coefficients shown in parentheses.

the largest pipelines had market power, in size or shares of deliveries, then they should have had higher price-cost margins that generated higher profit. That they did not, in a transition period, further erodes the "noncompetitive pipeline" rationale for regulation under the Natural Gas Act.

GAINS AND LOSSES FROM UNBUNDLING
AND PARTIAL DEREGULATION

Early in the restructuring process the new spot and futures markets were severely tested, and they performed better than had contract markets in bundled services under similar conditions in the mid-1970s. The severe winter of 1993–1994 in the Northeast and Midwest increased demands on the production and transport system, taking pipelines to the limits of their capacities. Spot and contract gas volumes were sufficient to clear markets, providing industrial customers and retail distributors with enough gas without having to cut off more than limited interruptible services. In fact, there was only "one major curtailment of firm gas transportation service during the mid-January freeze," and that resulted from an outage of an electricity generator that provided power to a pipeline.[19]

The high level of performance was due in part to increased use of in-ground storage. The shift of responsibility for service from the pipeline as merchant to the local distribution company buying its own gas at the wellhead had increased demands for high-deliverable storage close to final consumption points. In response, storage capacity increased, on schedule for adding 20 percent by the end of the 1990s.[20] As gas transported off-peak has increased, to be stored near the city gate to meet subsequent peak demands, seasonal variation in spot gas prices has for the most part disappeared.

Overall, however, gas reserves and gas production have not greatly expanded after Order 636. The replacement of merchant service by those of spot and futures markets in gas and transportation has basically altered all industry buy-sell relations. But in the first half of the 1990s, capacity to deliver gas and transport services to the city gate increased only by 15 percent, or less than 3 percent per annum (table 4.10).

More than one third of capacity came from expansion of the pipeline system out of Canada. With extensive new reserves and new pipelines operating under Canada's National Energy Board regulation, insofar as sales in the United States were concerned, Canadian sources have been outside the system of restructuring and renewed regulation in American markets.

Table 4.10. Interregional pipeline flow capacity, 1990 and 1996

Receiving region	Sending region	Capacity (mmcf/day) 1990	1996
Central	Canada	1,254	1,563
	Midwest	1,765	2,354
	Southwest	8,555	8,609
	Western	250	298
Total into region		**11,824**	**12,824**
Midwest	Canada	2,161	3,049
	Central	8,988	9,879
	Northeast	2,024	2,038
	Southeast	9,645	9,821
Total into region		**22,818**	**24,787**
Northeast	Canada	467	2,393
	Midwest	4,584	4,887
	Southeast	4,971	5,149
Total into region		**10,022**	**12,429**
Southeast	Northeast	100	520
	Southwest	19,801	20,846
Total into region		**19,901**	**21,366**
Southwest	Central	1,283	2,114
	Mexico	350	350
	Southeast	405	405
Total into region		**2,048**	**2,869**
Western	Canada	2,421	3,786
	Central	365	1,194
	Southwest	4,340	5,351
Total into region		**7,126**	**10,331**
Total within lower 48 states		**73,739**	**84,606**

Sources: Pipeline Capacity: EIAGIS-NG Geographic Information System, Natural Gas Pipeline State Border Capacity Database, as of December 1997.
Note: mmcf = million cubic feet.

The explanation for limited growth is that markets for spot gas and transport capacity have been constrained by Order 636. The development of firm capacity in existing pipelines has been limited by FERC price regulation of both firm and release capacity. Regulated prices on firm capacity have not determined transactions terms and conditions for use of that capacity (see table 4.3). But the use of capacity release has been limited by the regulatory constraint on bidders offering more than the FERC tariff price on firm capacity. These limits act like rent control in a housing market, creating disincentives to provide more capacity, whether by the pipeline or by the shipper in release contracts. By preventing markets from fully using available capacity, FERC regulation continues to impose rigidities in supply that were inherent in the merchant contract system of the 1970s and 1980s.

The limited capacity expansion of pipeline transportation has most likely worked through the market system adversely to affect prices and quantities. Actual prices for 1985 through 1994 are shown in table 4.11; starting at $2.10 per mcf, they fell to $1.20 per mcf in 1990 and to between $1.11 and $1.16 per mcf in three of the following five years. Production was close to 17 tcf initially but increased in the last two years by approximately 1 tcf per year.

These measures of performance differed greatly from what would have been realized had there been no regulation. Prices would have stabilized in the range

Table 4.11. Historical and model simulation prices, quantities, and reserves, 1985–1994

Year	Production (historical, tcf)	Production (supply-demand model simulation, tcf)	Reserves (historical, tcf)	Reserves (supply-demand model simulation, tcf)	Price index (historical, c/mmBtu, constant 1982 dollars)	Price index (supply-demand model simulation, c/mmBtu, constant 1982 dollars)
1985	16.15	22.38	167.99	243.83	210.58	99.50
1986	15.73	23.33	165.10	247.46	159.21	122.02
1987	16.28	23.55	163.94	242.37	132.53	104.03
1988	16.70	24.13	159.56	239.40	129.73	99.07
1989	16.91	24.49	163.82	234.16	123.96	93.77
1990	17.47	25.68	163.38	239.83	120.66	106.51
1991	17.34	25.82	165.42	239.87	111.65	101.33
1992	17.43	25.90	162.72	237.61	114.95	101.38
1993	17.70	26.18	161.08	235.29	132.23	98.30
1994	18.40	26.97	157.57	234.48	116.72	106.52

Sources: EIA historical statistics; DOE/EIA 1996; model simulations that establish equilibrium unregulated price index and quantity, as explained in the text.
Notes: [1] In chained 1982 cents, calculated using GDP implicit price deflators.
[2] Converted from c/mcf to c/mmBtu using dry production heat content.
[3] Represents price of gas sold and delivered by local distribution companies and does not reflect gas transported for the others.
[4] Reserves are at beginning of year.

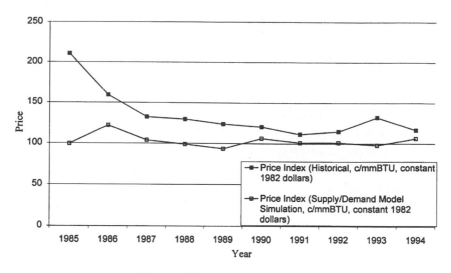

Figure 4.1. The price of gas, 1985–1994

from 98 cents to $1.06 per mcf over the period (as estimated for the price index in the supply-and-demand model for market clearing without regulation; see table 4.11). Production would have stabilized at 25–27 tcf per annum over the period 1990–1994, with three years in excess of 25 tcf and two years at 26–27 tcf. These relationships are illustrated in figures 4.1 and 4.2. Actual market prices, subject to partial deregulation under FERC, were higher, and production was lower, than what would have been realized in open markets without FERC controls.

The regulatory constraints on pipeline service prices restrict the development of pipeline capacity as a matter of course, and producers restrict the development of reserves given present and likely future pipeline capacity. This reduces the supply of gas at the wellhead and increases prices.

The gains and losses from this process are illustrated in figure 4.3. Actual wellhead prices for gas are set by reduced supplies (shown as S') clearing ongoing industrial and residential demands (demand function D) at the index price level P. The level of realized production is shown by Q. But without regulatory controls at the pipeline level, wellhead supply would be as shown by S, and the market clearing index price would be P^* for production Q^*. The price under partial deregulation is higher for lower production.

The gains at the higher price occur to producers with total increased revenues as indicated by the price difference times actual quantity (area A). But

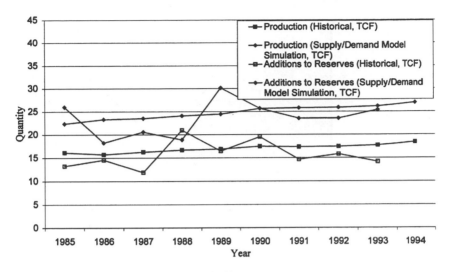

Figure 4.2. Production and additions to reserves, 1985–1994

the producers lose net returns that would have been forthcoming from additional sales if there were no regulation to both producers and pipelines (area *C*). Consumers lose area *A* from having to pay higher prices and also lose surplus that would have resulted from the additional output following from deregulation (area *B*).

Given realized prices and quantities and those simulated from the supply-and-demand model for unregulated markets, no one gained. Producer gains of $54.7 billion over the nine years from 1985 through 1994 were more than eclipsed by losses of $62.3 billion on reduced sales in that period. Consumers lost $66.7 billion from prices that were too high and quantities that were too low relative to those that would have resulted from unregulated markets for gas and transportation (table 4.12).

The partial deregulation of transport markets has created the third experiment, no-gain result. The behavior of spot gas prices at market hubs indicates that transportation has become sufficiently competitive to warrant the elimination of rate regulation. That regulation has had perverse results: the growth of capacity of the pipeline system in its newly integrated network configuration has been reduced, resulting in gas prices that have been high and production that has been low relative to what could have been realized in unregulated markets.

The access to transportation established by FERC Order 636 did give inde-

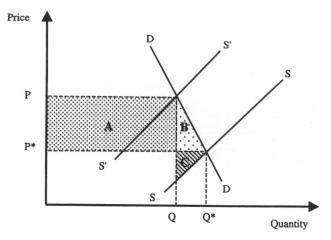

Figure 4.3. Gains and losses due to pipeline regulation

Table 4.12. Gains and losses of producers and pipelines from continued regulation, 1985–1994

	Method of estimation	Estimated 1982 dollars (in millions)
Losses of consumers who received production at prices higher than market clearing prices.	Difference between market clearing and regulated prices multiplied by historic production. (Area *A*)	54,777
Gains of pipelines from providing service at higher market clearing levels.	Difference between market clearing and regulated prices multiplied by historic production. (Area *A*)	54,777
Losses of consumers from decreased consumption due to higher prices.	Difference between regulated and market clearing price times difference between regulated and market clearing production divided by two. (Area *B*)	12,012
Loss of pipelines because of reduced capacity.	Difference between market clearing price and service price at historic throughput multiplied by the difference between regulated and market clearing throughput divided by two. (Area *C*)	62,326

Source: As explained in the text and derived from supply-demand model simulations.

pendent gas shippers the opportunity to move gas between major hubs through three or more pipelines. Because shippers have had access to competitive transportation, rate caps should be removed for all transport services between these major hubs, including both firm (primary and released) capacity. The question then would be whether regulation should continue on transportation beyond hubs where service is noncompetitive. The answer is that regulators should replicate the behavior on services between major hubs that have been deregulated. After FERC has removed tariff rates on released and firm capacity between major hubs, prices on those routes could be used to benchmark regulated tariffs between other city-pairs. Such benchmark rates would constrain any exercise of market power, if it still exists.

With complete deregulation, industry performance would improve. The transition to unregulated markets would add to performance as measured in terms of increased production, in the range of 25 tcf per annum. The current paradox resulting from regulation is that it constrains supply by causing low growth in transport capacity in the interior of the hub network. The pipelines offering unbundled firm transportation charge either the regulated tariff or lower negotiated rates. Because the tariff rate is capped by a formula based on average historical cost, and the negotiated rate is lower, the pipelines do not receive revenues sufficient to recover historical costs; they cannot undertake capacity replacement and expansion. With continued regulation, there are going to be continued constraints on the growth of pipeline capacity. The industry has to realize reductions in gas throughput and higher prices for delivered gas. The paradox leaves both producers and consumers worse off with regulated prices that are too high.

Chapter 5 The Unbundling
of Local Gas Retail Markets

Since the mid-1990s, a number of state regulatory initiatives have sought to bring "the benefits of competition" to retail customers in local gas markets. The retail gas-plus-distribution service of local utilities has been separated into two services, gas ownership and gas distribution, to allow residential and commercial customers to purchase gas from out-of-state suppliers and have that gas distributed separately by the local utility. Industrial customers buying at the wellhead have been able to separate gas from distribution since the late 1970s. But now many state regulatory agencies, by eliminating the local utility merchant function to create open access to local distribution systems, have taken FERC Order 636's unbundling of wholesale services to the retail burner tip of households and commercial customers.

As of March 2000, twenty-three states plus the District of Columbia had implemented programs that would allow some small retail customers—either residential or commercial or both—unbundled options comparable to those available to large industrial customers. These programs have varied from experiment to the requirement to remove local distribution companies entirely from the gas sales function.[1] Yet in spite of all this activity, small customer direct gas procurement has been limited. The pathbreaking programs in California and New York attracted few independent providers of separate gas supply service for the residential market, with the result that home and small business customer participation accounts for no more than a few percentage points of all customers. A few city-centered programs, offered as state experiments, have reached a high percentage of consumers but have been limited geographically. A nationwide initiative toward unbundled services by Enron Capital and Trade Corporation disappeared after a mid-1998 decision to pull out of residential energy markets. Nationwide, only about 4 percent of residential customers eligible to participate had chosen to do so.

Given that numerous programs are new or at the experimental stage, it is early to ask whether such fundamental structural changes at the retail level make gas markets more efficient and responsive to consumers. We can determine, however, in a preliminary examination of these markets, whether residential and small commercial customers can possibly benefit from unbundling markets for retail gas and distribution. The slow growth of customers seeking unbundling may indicate that consumer gains from making more gas suppliers available may not be substantial, and the high transaction costs inherent in unbundling may cancel out any such gains. Unbundling, initiated as a step to provide "the benefits from competition," may not involve net gains for those in whose name the effort is being undertaken.

STATE REGULATION OF RETAIL
GAS DISTRIBUTION

In most states, state regulatory agencies, similar to the Federal Power Commission or the Federal Energy Regulatory Commission, have oversight of price and service offerings of retail distribution companies for natural gas sold to households and most commercial establishments. Local investor-owned distribution companies and municipal utilities deliver more than two-thirds of end-use customer volumes. Intrastate pipelines, also regulated by the states, deliver almost 20 percent of natural gas through systems that combine transmission and distribution. The interstate pipelines regulated by FERC deliver less than 10 percent of supplies directly to end-use customers (table 5.1).

Certain classes of customers have complete dependency on the local distribution companies. Almost 90 percent of supplies to residential customers and more than 87 percent of supplies to commercial customers are delivered by dis-

Table 5.1. Sales and transport of natural gas volumes to final consumers

Distribution companies	63.8%
Municipal utilities	3.9%
Interstate pipelines	8.9%
Intrastate pipelines	18.8%
Other	4.6%
Total	100%

Source: EIA-176 company filings; data for 1996.

tribution utilities with state-franchised monopolies. For industrial customers, many with access to the interstate transmission pipelines, approximately 50 percent of their gas is delivered by a local distribution company. Even for gas used by electric generation companies, close to one third is delivered by local distribution companies (table 5.2).

These local distribution companies are regulated by state agencies, not by the Federal Energy Regulatory Commission, on any transaction, whether wholesale or retail, as long as the service does not cross state boundaries.[2] Under the Hinshaw Amendment of 1954 to the Natural Gas Act, state agencies have jurisdiction over pricing by distribution companies located within the state on bundled gas and delivery service or on the transportation of gas for others.

Federal and state regulation are fundamentally different in how they control prices for service. Exceptions include Texas, where intrastate pipelines are regulated by a state agency in a manner similar to federally regulated interstate

Table 5.2. Sources of sales and transport of natural gas (percentage)

	Residential	Commercial (including natural gas vehicles)	Industrial nonelectric	Industrial-cogeneration	Generation
Local distribution companies	89.2	87.3	49.1	54.1	33.9
Municipal utilities	5.5	5.6	3.4	0.5	1.2
Interstate pipelines	0.3	0.9	11.7	17.5	23.7
Intrastate pipelines	1.5	2.1	29.8	21.4	38.0
Other	3.5	4.0	6.0	6.5	3.2
Total	100.0	100.0	100.0	100.0	100.0

Source: EIA-176 company filings; data for 1996.

pipelines, and California, where the large retail distribution companies have long-distance pipelines and local distribution systems, which lead to some regulatory processes similar to those for the interstate pipelines.[3] But most states regulate local gas distribution companies, with low-pressure delivery lines that serve large numbers of small weather-sensitive residential and commercial customers, with cost-of-service justification of prices rather than price caps.

The state agencies have granted local franchise monopolies to each distributor to serve all or almost all potential consumers in the franchise area. The service coverage can be expanded to "almost all" if residential prices are kept as low as is consistent with covering costs of all service in the long run. However, as indicated, local distribution companies also serve half the national industrial load and a third of electric generation gas-burning capacity. To keep residential rates low, many state agencies have at times agreed to distributor initiatives to increase rates to the large industrial customers, and this has led to fuel switching and the bypassing of the local distributor.

Another difference between interstate pipelines and local distribution companies is in the nature of their contracts with customers. Interstate pipelines operated earlier for the most part with the expectation that they would fill their lines with their own gas or, later, after unbundling contracts, with the gas of independent shippers. Although pipelines have recently been constructed as at-risk facilities—that is, without regulation to ensure recovery of expenditures on capital—the relationship between the pipeline and customer is still contractually fixed. The pipelines no longer have open-ended merchant service agreements, but they continue to have an obligation to serve all potential customers that tap into their lines to the extent that space is available. In contrast, local distribution companies have had regulator-defined exclusive franchises and an explicit obligation to serve all customers, or at least all residential customers, within that franchise region. If a local distribution company is unable to meet total demand on its distribution network, then its tariff would define curtailments based on customer priority classes and not on terms and conditions in agreements with individual customers.

State regulators have generally regulated prices on the principle of allowing prices sufficient to recover costs of service. In practice, however, this rule has been distorted to allow prices in excess of direct costs for some services and prices below costs for others. Because of the mix of consumers and in order to set low prices for numerous small household customers, cost allocations have been weighted heavily toward industrial services in state regulation. The total revenues from distribution services have been set to cover non-gas costs for a forward-looking test year. In addition, purchase costs of gas and charges for interstate transportation have had to be passed through to final customers. This "revenue requirement" has been designed to provide the utility with the opportunity to earn a competitive return on investment. States such as California and New York allocate the requirement based on marginal costs of service plus the total costs of specific facilities that provide service to only that class. Other states allocate fewer costs to residential consumers, shifting those costs onto industrial consumers to the extent that competition of other fuels makes it feasible.

The resulting rate structure contains less variation across consumer groups than it would if regulation was intended to provide efficient price signals for passing through costs of service. Even though gas distributors have been subject to relatively higher demands for peak winter usage, relative rates on peak have not been increased to compensate for investments to provide for such increases. Regulated rates continue to be quite uniform over the year. Within a class, rates generally increase with volume even though unit costs decrease with volume, so that the distributor's margins are higher on services to more intensive users, a policy that only invites the bypassing of the distributor as these large users deal directly with the pipelines. Embedded in the revenue requirement are subsidies for various programs, including providing service to low-income customers, supporting weatherization campaigns, and enhancing gas conservation. All of these elements of rate structure may move toward satisfying certain regulatory goals, such as favoring interest groups, but they result in prices that give large users incentives to leave the distribution system.

Although state regulators have discussed "market-sensitive" pricing that would have the potential of keeping large industrial and commercial buyers on existing systems, they have generally persisted with practices that set prices too low for household consumers and too high for industrial-commercial consumers. In Texas, regulatory control of local distribution companies is still based on traditional cost allocation, primarily by local agencies, but intrastate pipelines are regulated by a state agency. California has allowed discounting from tariff rates for industrial customer transportation, but it still requires substantial regulatory review of the resulting discount contracts to determine whether the discounts "shift" costs to residential customers. A number of states have been experimenting with what they term "incentive" ratemaking, the determination of maximum allowable year-to-year changes in the level of rates. The resulting rates still have been initialized on cost-of-service calculations and have allocated costs traditionally. Rate increases may be capped, but the starting point has been a level based on cost of service.

THE RATIONALE FOR UNBUNDLING
AND RESTRUCTURING

Retail unbundling consists of separating the delivery of gas from transportation and from storage. The separated services are provided by independent companies, along with services such as storage, billing, and customer repair services. With unbundling comes the promise of deregulation: unbundled services could be purchased from sources not subject to rate regulation of a state regulatory agency. But there would be one significant exception; the distributor would still be required to obtain regulatory approval for construction and, in operations, for transportation services in its pipes to the burner tip.

The competitive benefits from unbundling are supposed to include cost savings and customer gains from increased choice among suppliers. There has been no empirical foundation for the position that vertical separation of gas ownership, transport, and billing reduces costs; indeed, there would be an increase in transaction costs with more transactions. But even if cost savings turn out to be nonexistent, competitive suppliers conceivably provide more different and even more innovative services. Although no proof has been provided for that proposition either, and even though it can apply to every industry to some degree, it is worth investigating in retail gas distribution. As markets become more efficient in the accumulation and use of information, with new contracts able to reduce or spread risk, then in the presence of constant change in gas costs and demands, gas plus transportation merchant systems based on long-term obligations to deliver at fixed prices become an anachronism. Customers may not want uniform service as selected by the regulator and they should be offered the opportunity to choose the level of service they desire. Traditional use of cost of service pricing, with prices of distribution averaged across consumer groups, impedes supplier decision making to take advantage of cost and demand differences.

Yet this case for unbundling and partial deregulation is not provable. The transaction costs created by unbundling are potentially large, particularly for small customers, as each becomes a participant in wellhead and regional hub markets for gas on spot or futures contracts. To avoid these markets, small customers deal with brokers or independent service companies that bundle services. Open access to separate gas and distribution could cost more in search and transaction expenditures than the benefits from improved service quality. If so, then markets will evolve until providers are down to one or two offering service and consumers will use the local utility for gas-plus-distribution.

Furthermore, the economic theory behind unbundling is faulty. Dividing services into separate layers of providers will not create a competitive retail market when there is monopoly in any one layer. It will lead to more regulation to define the layers and limit prices at the "bottleneck" layer. Some will have the characteristics of a natural monopoly so that competition will not develop in spite of the best intentions of those mandating the restructuring. Providing unbundled services to end users, even without increased transaction costs, still results in a regulated price.

What groups, then, are the potential gainers or losers? Distributors could gain because unbundling could conceivably reduce their costs of regulation. Purchased gas costs would be passed through to customers, so that they would not have to appeal to the state regulatory agency for rate increases to cover increased purchase costs. Because too large a share of utility system costs have arguably been charged to industrial customers, which has made industrial rates noncompetitive, any new approach by which unbundled transportation was provided at uniform per mcf prices would allow retail utilities to compete with bypass pipelines for industrial customers. But unbundling services to large industrial customers endangers the retail distributors' capacity to serve as the suppliers of last resort. That part of the revenue requirement previously met with relatively higher price-cost margins on industrial customer deliveries has to be replaced with increased earnings generated by higher prices to residential customers. These customers could be losers from the higher prices, if granted, or from the cutbacks in peak period services, if not granted by the state regulatory agency.

UNBUNDLED SERVICE OPTIONS FOR SMALL
RETAIL GAS CUSTOMERS

Results from providing unbundled services for small customers are extremely limited. Many states have created programs by which retail commercial customers aggregate load to contract for large-volume distributor delivery services, but few customers have participated, given that interest has been limited. California created unbundled transportation-only tariffs for all retail customers in 1992. Since then, less than 4 percent of California's retail volume has been in aggregation programs, and most of that has been from the larger commercial customers, such as supermarkets and fast-food outlet chains.

Some state agencies have initiated pilot programs in which the utility has offered gas services through an independent subsidiary. Initiating such a program has involved extensive advertising and public education to achieve low-level market penetration. In all but one case the most successful so-called alternative provider was an independent subsidiary of the local distribution company. As a result, a number of states, such as Wisconsin, have not continued beyond the initial program, citing limited benefits to end use customers as registered in widespread consumer disinterest.

From the perspective of "benefits," those for residential customers of alternate supply sources to date have turned out to be less evident than for industrial gas consumers. Residential customers have not shown interest even after new providers have made large investments in advertising. This indifference on the part of customers may reflect continued ignorance about new options, or it may reflect a sense that the benefits from using alternate suppliers are small and the reliability of delivery is unknown from sources other than the utility. Moreover, the state agencies promoting retail unbundling have not been able to show consumers gains from unbundling. There are seventeen ongoing programs for which agency documentation on results is available. Only four have indicated positive gains to consumers; none has documented costs of transactions, delay, or variations in service quality (see table 5.3).

From the distributors' perspective, the potential for service offerings from unbundling services to small customers is much less than it is to industrial customers. The complication for the distributor is in provision of peak load services, the costs of which would have to be recovered in prices for standby service. Those prices would not differ from prices for merchant service, except that the charge for gas would be passed through not at the city gate but at the burner tip. But to date, the state regulatory process has not established a bright line between peak load services to remain with the distribution company and services to be opened up to others. Alternative suppliers could provide baseload levels of flowing gas, and the local utility could provide peak load gas supply. But that need not be the case. Independent marketers could expand into managing reliability and could meet peak demands through withdrawals from their own storage or from spot purchases in day-to-day gas markets. Extensive proceedings will be required to define the line between competitive supply and utility peaking services.

Table 5.3. Costs and benefits of unbundling natural gas services to residential customers

Program	Start date	Number of customers	Benefit–cost	Comments, description
California				
Statewide program; limited participation (under 5%); revisions with PG&E's Gas Accord designed to increase participation	1993	All eligible; <5% elected	n/a	Statewide tariffs established 1996
Florida				
People's Gas Company Teco approved 12/13/96, extended 2/10/98 with modifications	1/1/97	230,000	+	Staff believes that People's aggregation program has resulted in lower costs to the pilot program customers and should be expanded to include more customers (1/1/98 Staff Rpt., Div. of Legal Services; PSC-96-1515OF-GU).
Georgia				
Atlanta Gas Light (AGL)	11/1/98	All eligible	n/a	AGL filed under legislation giving utilities the right to become transport only. Utility charges SFV rates, maintains interstate capacity and peaking facilities. Large marketers (Enron, PG&E ES, Sonat) withdrew from residential market 9/14/98 before date to trigger assignment of customers.
Maryland				
Washington Gas Light 2-year pilot	10/15/96	—	15%	Marketers offered percentage; guaranteed fixed discount.
Massachusetts				
Bay State Year 1; Year 2	11/1/96; 11/1/97	—	$750,600; $120,000	

New Jersey				
New Jersey Natural Gas (NJNG) pilot in Monmouth, Ocean, and Morris Counties	1/2/98	<30,000; approx. 10% of market	—	Savings result from several factors. Suppliers are not subject to the same taxes as utilities, like NJNG, so the tax of the sale of gas is lower for a supplier.
New Jersey Natural Energy (NJNE), the marketing affiliate of NJNG offer NJNG customers	—	—	$625,000	Sample offer: $125 signing bonus for first 5,000, plus match utility regulated prices; can donate bonus to charity (NJ Resources press release, 1/5/98).
PSE&G (compete for NJNG customers' gas sales in first pilot)	3/10/97	5,000 eligible	—	Sample offer: $0.35/therm, 13% decrease over current total gas bill; locked for 1 year (PSE&G press release, 3/10/97).
Public Service Electric and Gas pilot approved 3/12/97 for Piscataway, Bloomfield, Pennsaken, and Westhampton through June 1998	5/1/97	65,000 eligible	—	18,000 out of 180,000 commercial and industrial have opted for transport since 1/1/95.
New York				
Choice for all customers implemented 1996 New York PSC staff report 10/4/97	Fall 1996	11,000 elected	—	Statewide at mid '97; 3% of small customer firm sales switched to transport; 35% of those residential.
Ohio				
Columbia Gas of Ohio greater Toledo pilot	4/1/97	170,000 eligible; 60,000 elected	$8 million	49,000 (30.1%) of 158,500 eligible residential customers; 5,310 (46.2%) of small commercial.

(continued)

Table 5.3. Continued

Program	Start date	Number of customers	Benefit–cost	Comments, description
Customer Choice; statewide	8/1/98	1,300,000	—	15 suppliers, new enrollees 3–5,000/month; comprehensive LDC education program, from press release 6/18/98.
Pennsylvania				
Columbia Gas of PA Allegheny and Washington Counties	11/1/97	137,000	—	Gas flow started Nov. 1, 1997; 10 certified marketers; print, broadcast ads; public meetings (press release, 7/10/97).
Columbia Gas of PA Washington County pilot	1996–97	37,000 eligible; 5,400 elected	+	Consumers who participated in the Washington pilot last year shaved as much as 10 percent off their monthly gas costs (President and CEO Gary J. Robinson noted; press release, 7/10/97).
Energy Select Phase I	—	19,300 eligible; 15,600 elected	—	18-month test; mailings, town meetings (National Fuel press release, 6/12/97).

CONCLUSION

Even when unbundling has been limited to flowing supply, regulators have invoked requirements for utility line access, system balancing, and load forecasting. In one program, residential unbundling has led to the definition and separation of the residential rate into twenty-seven separately priced service components in the consumer's bill. More basic, distribution line capacity and storage to meet peak demands in extreme weather conditions have to meet regulatory standards. In a market framework, with unbundling, the state agency has not allowed the incumbent distributor to curtail small customers if a competitive suppler defaults; the utility remains the supplier of last resort. If alternative suppliers provide more than flowing baseload gas, the role of the utility will have to be redefined. Multiple suppliers will have to handle varying load, and regulation of the incumbent distributor will have to be restructured so that marketers could not take the most attractive customers, leaving the utility with those that are the highest cost to serve and the least willing to pay. The result otherwise is that unbundling to generate the "benefits of competition" creates the necessity of extensive further intervention in individual transactions by the state regulatory agency.

Chapter 6 Partial Deregulation and the Future Performance of Gas Markets

The regulatory moves to restructure and partially deregulate gas industry transactions over the past twenty years proceeded from the Natural Gas Policy Act of 1978 to FERC Order 636 to state agencies implementing retail unbundling. Gas ownership has been separated from transportation so that customers now buy transport and gas at the wellhead for delivery to the city gate. Local distribution is now at least partially separate from gas ownership, although still mostly provided to the consumer by the local gas utility. Gas prices have been decontrolled, but prices remain regulated for firm transportation services.

Given that the status quo is the product of partial deregulation, would comprehensive deregulation give the consumer a higher-value choice of gas suppliers and transporters? Would the services of deregulated transporters and distributors improve? The current political response is that deregulation is as complete as is possible within existing market institutions. Pipelines and retail distributors have established market positions not subject to new deregulatory incursions. Large sunk costs in installed networks constitute barriers to entry to competitive service providers. To restructure further would be to reduce the service package offered by the regulated transportation company to the minimum to be provided by this sunk cost infrastructure that still had to be price-controlled. For example, at retail, such revenue cycle services as billing and meter reading could go to independent service providers rather than remaining in the package provided by the incumbent gas distribution company because these services can be provided by numerous firms competitively. But that is all.

Additional services could be separated from distribution, but the results require that customers deal with additional supply entities. As many as a dozen gas providers at hub exchanges, half a dozen pipelines within fifty miles of the city gate, and more than one local distributor could all be involved in a transaction. Although the billing service provider could promise to serve as the consumer's agent, there are obvious increased transaction costs in delivery from numerous upstream gas and service providers. But the roadblock is that not all services provided by the retail utility when unbundled can be made competitive. Local distribution companies take on planning and investment functions to meet regulatory requirements for reliability, are the supplier of last resort of customer peak-day gas demands, and administer subsidized services to low-income residential customers. In most jurisdictions, they deliver to nonpaying customers during winter months. These services cannot be fragmented by current agency practice among alternative service providers; they could be eliminated but not delivered by numerous providers.

To indicate the extent of current last resort responsibilities, consider unbundling and restructuring of distribution. To meet peak demands of residential customers, the retail distributor makes decisions on its throughput based on its holdings of firm delivery capacity, access to storage, weather forecasts, and the servicing pipeline in-pipe inventory, or "line pack," over its service region. Under current regulatory practices, service to residential customers cannot be suspended when the demands of all customers at peak in extreme weather exceed volumetric throughput of gas. Under restructuring, residential customers willing to be cut off, perhaps as a result of paying lower prices, would in practice be cut off as pipeline system pressures decline. Other customers kept on the system would pay the peak price for their gas where that price would be twice or more the current off-peak price.

Given this scenario, for example, deregulation by unbundling and deaveraging prices on services to residential consumers is difficult to accept politically. The state regulatory agency and/or legislature ultimately has to end the process of restructuring when encountering the incumbent distributor with its underground line to the home or office building. There could be one or more sources of gas supply, and of billing and metering, but there would be only one gas line. To deregulate the buy-sell relationship between the pipeline and the distributor, and then the consumer and the distributor operating that line, is to complete the process. Adding companies in retail billing creates the appearance of competition, but still only a single entity controls the network to determine who gets the gas in the coldest month. The common distribution line would be used by a deregulated service provider to distribute services to those most willing to pay, not to all those who want service at last year's prices.

Would that make a difference to consumers in the long run? The local distribution service package has accounted for one fourth of the retail price (see table 2.2). Larger fractions have been accounted for by the wellhead and wholesale market prices. The question is whether it matters if deregulation of both transportation and distribution causes transportation and local distribution prices to decrease. There are obviously costs to consumers, but the gains could be greater. Simulations with the supply-and-demand model indicate possible magnitudes of gains for consumers. Two price series, over the years 1995 to 2010, for partial versus complete deregulation, when compared indicate very substantial net gains from complete deregulation throughout the entire industry.

FUTURE INDUSTRY PERFORMANCE
WITHOUT REGULATION

Demand is assumed to move along a growth path resulting from changes in the prices of coal, petroleum products, and electricity. These prices are assumed to follow the same process as in the historical period. The other variables that determine total demand—that is, industrial production and personal consumption—are assumed to increase at historical growth rates. Supply is generated by initial reserves and total wells, and by changes in oil prices and rates of take from existing wells.

An initial step in predicting the resulting future prices is to test for the stability of the determining variables—prices of fuels, industrial production, personal consumption expenditures, and initial reserves and total wells. This test is undertaken by applying regression analysis to the first differences of these variables (tables 6.1 and 6.2). Of the more than thirty coefficients, only twelve are significant; however, the adjusted R-square values indicate that the fit of the equations, for differences in variables, from 0.134 to 0.333, is superior for equa-

Table 6.1. Simulations of future prices: step 1, estimation of exogenous variables
as a function of endogenous variables

Regression equations

Dependent variable Description		ΔPC Change in Price of Coal	ΔPP Change in Price of Petroleum	ΔPE Change in Price of Electricity	ΔPCE Change in Personal Consumption Expenditure
Independent variable					
Name	Description				
Intercept	n/a	0.006353 (0.14)	−0.1475 (−0.54)	−0.03252 (−0.15)	34.37 (3.14)
ΔLPC	Change in Lagged Price of Coal	0.6249 (3.11)	0.02589 (0.02)	0.1806 (0.95)	n/a
ΔLPP	Change in Lagged Price of Petroleum	−0.0335 (−0.66)	0.5657 (1.83)	0.3154 (1.31)	n/a
ΔLPE	Change in Lagged Price of Electricity	−0.0222 (−0.52)	−0.1576 (−0.61)	0.3066 (1.52)	n/a
ΔLIP	Change in Lagged Industrial Production	0.02590 (2.26)	0.03574 (0.51)	0.04772 (0.88)	−8.751 (−3.05)
ΔLPCE	Change in Lagged Personal Consumption Expenditure	−0.001121 (−1.20)	0.001123 (0.20)	−0.002191 (−0.49)	0.7844 (4.11)
	Durbin m-statistic	−0.605	0.110	−1.28	−0.514
	Adjusted R-squared	0.238	0.134	0.333	0.321

Source: As explained in the text.

tions of that type, making the error in predicting future levels quite small (the
error in estimated reserves, for instance, would contribute 0.5 percent to the total reserves estimate each year).

The second step in predicting prices is to estimate one hundred alternative
scenarios for supply-and-demand equilibrium in the model for one hundred
sets of stipulated values of the determining variables. This makes it possible to
construct an error term "ϵ_s" for estimated values of market clearing price and
quantity.[1] The geometric means of gas price and quantity from the one hundred simulations, starting from both 1994 historical and 1994 "deregulation"
conditions, are shown in tables 6.3 and 6.4. In partially deregulated markets,

Table 6.2. Simulations of future prices: step 1, estimation of exogenous variables, continued

Regression equations					
Dependent variable		ΔCTGW	ΔIP	ED	RIE
Description		Change in Cumulative Gas Wells	Change in Industrial Production	Excess Demand	Reserves Identity Error
Independent variable					
Name	Description				
Intercept	n/a	2661.5 (2.37)	0.2035 (0.27)	−0.3542 (−1.89)	−0.8674 (−2.39)
ΔL	Change in Lagged Value of the Dependent Variable	0.5737 (3.80)	−0.3757 (−1.91)	n/a	n/a
L	Lagged Dependent Variable	n/a	n/a	0.6846 (4.81)	0.273 (1.54)
ΔLPCE	Change in Lagged Personal Consumption Expenditure	n/a	0.05149 (3.94)	n/a	n/a
Ticker	n/a	n/a	n/a	0.027 (2.44)	0.0385 (2.23)
	Durbin H-statistic	−1.463	0.775*	−1.864	0.121*
	Adjusted R-squared	0.303	0.309	0.853	0.312

Source: As explained in the text.
Note: *Durbin m-statistic presented whenever H-statistic is not defined.

prices decline in real terms over the next fifteen years (table 6.3), but in completely deregulated markets, they also decline, at a lower rate, but from a lower initial year level (table 6.4). Starting from the historical values, generated by partially deregulated markets, prices tend to be higher than when starting from complete deregulation. The reason for the difference is that, under partial deregulation, the industry has accumulated fewer reserves, so that the current equilibrium price for production is higher. The higher prices stimulate more wildcat and extension-revision activity that after a few years adds more to reserves, so that prices fall more rapidly after more reserves are accumulated. The difference in prices between the two scenarios is almost 60 percent in 1995 but

Table 6.3. Forecasts of prices, production, and reserves based
on continued regulation

Year	Real wellhead price* ($/mmBtu)	Standard deviation	Gas production (billions mmBtu)	Standard deviation	Gas reserves (billions mmBtu)	Standard deviation
1995	1.870	0.120	20.44	0.216	163.6	0.806
1996	1.448	0.225	22.13	0.394	181.9	2.777
1997	1.377	0.184	23.49	0.536	192.1	3.457
1998	1.301	0.194	24.68	0.758	200.1	4.464
1999	1.234	0.188	25.73	1.029	206.0	6.596
2000	1.188	0.189	26.67	1.371	210.0	8.643
2001	1.126	0.197	27.53	1.661	213.4	10.49
2002	1.091	0.199	28.28	1.946	215.0	12.15
2003	1.032	0.218	28.92	2.266	216.6	13.79
2004	1.017	0.221	29.50	2.538	216.6	16.46
2005	0.974	0.245	30.03	2.834	218.1	17.90
2006	0.968	0.246	30.63	3.183	218.0	20.25
2007	0.931	0.289	31.28	3.540	219.5	21.57
2008	0.893	0.284	31.84	3.891	219.4	25.00
2009	0.862	0.311	32.35	4.254	220.3	25.54
2010	0.844	0.341	32.85	4.707	219.6	29.41

Source: As explained in the text.
Note: *In 1982 dollars; simulations of future prices are initiated from historical values of all variables given continued regulation.

is less than 10 percent by the year 2010 (see both for predicted prices and production levels in fig. 6.2 and table 6.4).

Regulated and deregulated market behaviors converge in the second decade of the twenty-first century. The supply-dampening effects of regulation decrease over time and disappear, even in this industry in which investments have long lives. The current industry underinvestment in exploration and development, caused by pipeline price regulation, makes current prices higher, which then increases both development activities and production until the catch-up with unregulated markets is complete.

Regulation brought about a smaller gas production industry in the 1980s that continued to be smaller in the 1990s. But as more limited supply in the future clears markets at higher prices, investment will be added and reserves will be increased, which in turn will increase pipeline production. Even so, there are

Table 6.4. Forecasts of prices, production, and reserves assuming complete deregulation

Year	Real wellhead price* ($/mmBtu)	Standard deviation	Gas production (billions mmBtu)	Standard deviation	Gas reserves (billions mmBtu)	Standard deviation
1995	1.040	0.068	28.33	0.272	241.7	0.806
1996	1.010	0.082	28.79	0.404	240.3	2.704
1997	0.985	0.096	29.20	0.623	238.8	3.814
1998	0.977	0.119	29.61	0.920	237.1	5.077
1999	0.961	0.133	30.05	1.234	236.2	7.490
2000	0.953	0.145	30.48	1.616	235.3	9.796
2001	0.929	0.159	30.93	1.929	235.1	11.88
2002	0.918	0.168	31.34	2.230	234.0	13.89
2003	0.886	0.188	31.69	2.564	233.5	15.61
2004	0.883	0.197	32.03	2.834	232.0	18.36
2005	0.858	0.220	32.33	3.141	232.2	19.94
2006	0.859	0.226	32.75	3.506	231.1	22.29
2007	0.836	0.263	33.25	3.886	231.5	23.78
2008	0.808	0.263	33.66	4.255	230.7	27.07
2009	0.786	0.287	34.05	4.636	230.6	27.95
2010	0.775	0.318	34.43	5.105	229.6	31.29

Source: As explained in the text.
Note: *In 1982 dollars; simulations of future prices are initiated from values of all variables consistent with 1996 equilibrium of the supply-demand model with complete deregulation.

losses year to year. Under complete deregulation, production would grow on average at 1.31 percent per year, but it would grow at 3.21 percent per year for the status quo. Both scenarios predict price decline, at 1.94 percent with complete deregulation and 5.16 percent per year for continuation of the regulatory status quo. The "catch-up" process under regulation takes place because prices are too high and quantities are too low.

The dynamics of gas market regulation at all levels are such that the consumer does without substantial benefits. The difference between prices, over the years 1995–2010, generates on average $600 million in consumer losses currently (area *B* in fig. 4.3, net of any shift of returns from producer to consumer). This is because under regulation the wellhead equilibrium price now is $0.90 per mcf in constant 1982 dollars higher than it would be with deregulation.

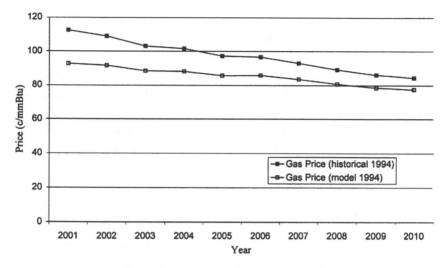

Figure 6.1. Future natural gas wellhead prices

CONCLUSION

The growth and development of the gas industry, even if free of natural disasters, will nevertheless be constrained by continued FERC and state agency regulation of transportation and distribution services. There is no analytical foundation for the argument that transportation has to continue to be regulated

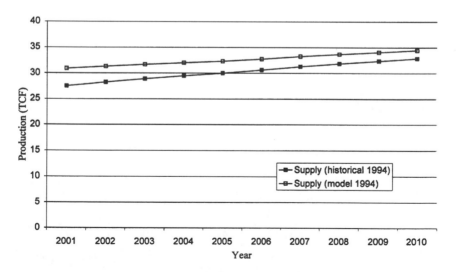

Figure 6.2. Future natural gas production rates by year

because it is noncompetitive. Transport prices do not have to be capped. State controls of distributors continue to constrain prices and unbundling service offerings is not a substitute for deregulation even if it were, contrary to indications, accepted by consumers. These regulatory practices keep prices too high, limit the growth of transportation capacity, and therefore ultimately limit production delivered to consumers.

Even so the industry should be able to overcome the negative results of intervention by the year 2010. Gas production and transport is moving toward long-term supply levels that are likely to be close to those realized if markets were free of regulation. But we need not wait that long, and indeed, we could realize prices today that are 20 percent less by eliminating current federal and state regulation of transmission and distributor systems. After forty years of regulation and twenty years of partial deregulation, at low-level performance, consumers would gain from deregulation and resulting lower prices at all levels of the industry.

Notes

CHAPTER 1: AN INTRODUCTION TO REGULATION
AND THE PERFORMANCE OF GAS MARKETS

1. On the responsibilities of the FPC, see 49 Stat. 847, 848, 851; 52 Stat. 822, consolidated in 16 U.S. Code §§ 792, 793, 797, 824; 15 U.S. Code § 717b.

2. See *Fed. Power Comm'n v. N. Natural Gas Co.,* 346 U.S. 922 (1954), as an example of how regulatory limits on prices were calculated with regard to natural gas pipeline firms.

3. *S.C. Generating Co.,* in 16 *Federal Power Commission Reports* (hereafter cited as *FPC*) 52, 58 (1956).

4. *In the Matter of Kan. Pipe Line & Gas Co. and N.Dak. Consumers Gas Co.* 2 *FPC* 29 (1939).

5. *Phillips Petroleum Co. v. Wis.,* 347 U.S. 672 (1954).

6. See President's Advisory Council on Executive Organization 1971.

7. FPC 1971.

8. See MacAvoy 1962, ch. 3, for an early discussion of pipeline economics; subsequent analysis can be found in *Pacific Gas Transmission Co. et al.,* 42 *FPC* 1046 (1969).

9. The Atlantic Seaboard Formula is given in *Atlantic Seaboard Corporation et al.,* in 94 (N.S.) *Public Utilities Report* 245 (1952). The costs C assigned to service j are: $Cj = VCj + (K/2) [Qj/(Qi + Qj)] + (K/2) [Qjt/(Qit + Qjt)]$, where VC is total variable cost actually incurred in j, K is total capital costs,

and Q refers to volumes consumed by j and other i demanders throughout the year as well as during peak load period t.

10. Federal expenditures for natural gas pipeline regulation are shown as $3.526 million in fiscal year 1968 according to Bureau of Budget 1970, 930.

11. Compiled from regulatory expenses and consultants' charges reported by the interstate pipeline companies on FPC Form 2, *Annual Report for Natural Gas Companies.* Allowing for reporting omissions and errors in allocating costs, the range was probably $2–$3 million.

12. *Permian Basin Area Rate Cases,* 390 U.S. 747 (1968).

13. See ibid. and *Permian Basin Area Rate Proceeding et al.* (hereafter cited as *Permian Basin Proceeding*), 34 *FPC* 159 (1965), Docket No. AR 61-l.

14. This estimate is based on statistics given in FPC 1969, 55–56. Technically speaking, price increase requests were classified by the commission as suspended for five months after receipt, during which time the party making a request was enjoined from charging the proposed higher price. After five months the party could then put the higher price into effect. Any revenue increase collected, however, was subject to refund to the extent that it resulted from exceeding the ceiling rate allowed by the commission. With seven thousand rates in suspension, considerable uncertainty and delay ensued.

15. *Permian Basin Proceeding,* 197. In the same sources, see also the testimony of S. F. Sherwin, Exhibit 42-J (SFS-1), Schedule 17, Docket Nos. AR 64-1 and AR 64-2. The estimates offered here include the costs of certification and of rate schedule review and so should not be attributed to area proceedings alone.

16. Producer commitments to interstate pipelines are given in the FPC's annual reports. See especially FPC 1970.

17. Gerwig 1962, 69–92, and MacAvoy 1970, 281, suggest a range from $10 million to $58 million for opportunity costs incurred through regulatory delay. The working figure is 0.17 cents per mcf per month of delay, allowing alternatives for a one-month delay or a six-month delay.

18. FPC 1970, table 5, xiii.

CHAPTER 2: A MODEL OF NATURAL GAS MARKET WELLHEAD PRICES AND QUANTITIES

1. This procedure is appropriate for estimating gas demand in the residential, commercial, and industrial sectors. The demand in the electric utility sector, however, is the sum of the demands for electricity in the industrial, commercial, and residential sectors. After calculating the amounts of fuels used to produce that electricity, the procedure is then the same as that for industrial demand.

2. On the supply side, described below, they are the price of gas (PG) and percentage changes in the price of gas (SPG) and in the total gas wells (STGW).

The average price of outstanding contracts on which there is production is the price used here. However, there might be problems with that price in a regression analysis of supply and demand. Both supply and demand should react to the prices in new contracts, not on the average price of all contracts. But the problem of using averages is not as serious as it seems at first. The proportion of "new" and "old" contracts has changed slowly over time, at least up to 1985. In the 1960s and early 1970s it remained constant, with old expiring contracts being substituted by new contracts with same contractual obligations and prices. The shortages of the 1970s then brought forth a higher proportion of new contracts (total natural gas consumption remained stable in that period) at significantly higher prices. In the surplus period, new contract prices departed more rapidly from old contract prices, but only a small percentage of gas moved under the new contracts. In the 1990s, the largest percentage of volumes moved were in spot agreements for spot prices, which constitute most of the average. As a result, both the price in new contracts and the average price increased significantly. The correlation between the two prices was high, or at least has been when small samples of new contract prices have been made available.

3. The test of forecast reliability of this model is to determine whether the error terms in the regression equations contain serial correlation—that is, whether or not for error term e_t = $\rho e_{t-1} + v_t$. If error terms are serially correlated, so that $\hat{\rho} \gtrless 0$, then the reliability of equation estimators is reduced. The test for serial correlation, introduced by Durbin 1970, tests for serial correlation using the h-statistic: $h \equiv \rho \sqrt{\dfrac{T}{1 - T(Var\,b)}}$, where $\hat{\rho}$ is the estimated value of the coefficient of serial correlation, T is the sample size, and $Var\,b$ is the square of the standard error of the regression coefficient of the lagged dependent variable. Under the null hypothesis of no serial correlation, this h-statistic is distributed as a standard normal random variable; however, it is not defined when $Var\,b \geq$ $1/T$. A test for serial correlation under this condition is Durbin's m-test, which is based on a regression analysis of the equation $e_t = a + b_1 Y_{t-1} + b_2 X_{1t} + b_3 X_{2t} + \ldots + \rho^* e_{t-1}$, where Y_{t-1} is the lagged dependent variable, X_{it} is the ith independent variable, and e is the residual from the original regression equation. The m-test consists of testing the null hypothesis $\rho^* = 0$, using Student's t-statistic. This statistic is shown for the relevant equations in the supply-and-demand model. In each instance the null hypothesis cannot be rejected. See Berndt 1991.

4. Note that production equals consumption plus storage and pipeline use of gas. See the sources of data for tables 2.1 and following.

CHAPTER 3: THE REGULATION OF GAS FIELD
CONTRACTS AND THE RESULTING GAINS AND
LOSSES FROM MARKET PERFORMANCE

1. *Phillips Petroleum Co. v. Wis.,* 347 U.S. 672 (1954).
2. Pierce and Gellhorn 1994, 5.
3. MacAvoy 1965.
4. Supporters of the act were not saddened by the fact that the transport rates actually increased as a result of government intervention (rates between hubs increased, so that intermediate points would not be served at rates on short-haul traffic that were higher than rates on long-haul traffic passing through the same hubs). Eastern region shippers would

pay 30 cents for the shipment of 100 pounds of grain, as long as westerners were paying no less than that. The railroads were satisfied that prices were more stable *and* higher. See MacAvoy 1965, ch. 5.

5. The patterns established in dealing with railroads were repeated in regulating telecommunications (1910, ICC), electric power generation and distribution (1920, FPC), and later natural gas transportation (1938, FPC). See Cushman 1941; and Breyer and Mac-Avoy 1974.

6. *Smyth v. Ames,* 169 U.S. 466 (1898). It is interesting to see the reversal in argumentation of the parties involved as the history unfolded. Initially, consumer advocates were in favor of using "fair" value of inputs, because they feared that business owners would use unreliable historical records to set prices too high. Decades later, after regulations and the Securities and Exchange Commission made record keeping a much more reliable and transparent process, businesses became the advocates of "fair value" concept because a backward-looking, historic-based accounting process did not reflect their expected future expenditures and therefore made it difficult to attract financing on capital markets.

7. *Fed. Power Comm'n v. Hope Natural Gas Co.* (hereafter cited as *FPC v. Hope*), 320 U.S. 591 (1944).

8. FPC 1956, 106–107.

9. *Phillips Petroleum Co. v. Wis.,* 347 U.S. 672 (1954)

10. An additional restriction on producers was the ruling by the FPC that any gas reserve from an identifiable field that was sold to an interstate pipeline at any time was under federal regulation for the life of that reserve.

11. *Phillips Petroleum Co. v. Wis.,* 347 U.S. 672 (1954).

12. 15 U.S.C.S. Sec. 717e.

13. Establishing the rate base B has been contentious, if not as much so as setting the rate of return r. The commission has had to decide if company assets were "used and useful" as well as whether "prudence" was exercised in decisions to construct or install specific assets. See Pierce and Gellhorn 1994, 102.

14. If technological progress affected all segments of the industry, the second problem directly affected only producers. We will see later how this changed the dynamics of the industry in the 1960s and 1970s.

15. Foreshadowing future problems, Justice Jackson noted in his extensive dissenting opinion in *FPC v. Hope,* "To make a fetish of mere accounting is to shield from examination the deeper causes, forces, movements, and conditions which should govern rates. Even as a recording of current transactions, bookkeeping is hardly an exact science. As a representation of the condition and trend of a business, it uses symbols of certainty to express values that actually are in constant flux. It may be said that in commercial or investment banking or any business extending credit success depends on knowing what not to believe in accounting. Few concerns go into bankruptcy or reorganization whose books do not show them solvent and often even profitable. If one cannot rely on accountancy accurately to disclose past or current conditions of a business, the fallacy of using it as a sole guide to future price policy ought to be apparent" (320 U.S. 643 [1944]).

16. See Mulherin 1986, 109.

17. See FPC, Bureau of Natural Gas 1972.

18. The percentage of total consumption by residential and commercial buyers was 45 percent in 1962 and 43 percent in 1968; as the natural gas shortage appeared on the horizon, the percentage of residential consumption increased. See FPC, *Statistics of Interstate Natural Gas Pipelines* (annual); see also Breyer and MacAvoy 1973, 977ff.

19. The amount remaining to be discovered had been estimated as 851 tcf by both the National Petroleum Council (U.S. Department of the Interior, National Petroleum Council, 1971, tables 291 and 293, p. 367) and by the University of Colorado Mineral Resources Institute's Potential Gas Committee (Potential Gas Committee 1971). A later report by the Potential Gas Committee, issued in December 1973, gives 1,146 tcf. A U.S. Geological Survey circular estimated the remaining amount at 2,100 tcf, with a range of estimates between 1,178 and 6,600 tcf (U.S. Department of the Interior, U.S. Geological Survey, 1973). Of course, the amount actually found and put in the reserves category would depend on the level of exploratory activity, on costs of development, and on the prices offered by the pipeline buyers.

20. James M. Landis was particularly critical of the FPC's performance in the field of natural gas regulation, charging it with delays so egregious as to indicate disregard of the consumer interest. He wrote: "The FPC without question represents the outstanding example of the breakdown of the administrative process. The complexity of its problems is no answer to its more than patent failures. These failures relate primarily to the natural gas field. These defects stem from attitudes of the unwillingness of the Commission to assume its responsibilities under the Natural Gas Act and its attitudes . . . of refusing in substance to obey the mandates of the Supreme Court of the United States and other federal courts. The Commission has exhibited no inclination to use powers that it possesses to get abreast of its docket. . . . The recent action of the Commission on September 28, 1960 in promulgating area rates . . . has come far too late to protect the consumer. . . . The Commission's past inaction and past disregard of the consumer interest has led the States to seek to force it to discharge its responsibilities. . . . Delay after delay in certifications and the prescription of rates has cost the public millions of dollars. . . . The Commission has literally done nothing to reduce the delays which have constantly increased. . . . The dissatisfaction with the work of the Commission has gone so far that there is a large measure of agreement on separating from the Commission its entire jurisdiction over natural gas and creating a new commission to handle these problems exclusively. . . . Primarily leadership and power must be given to its Chairman, and qualified and dedicated members with the consumer interest at heart must be called into service to correct what has developed into the most dismal failure in our time of the administrative process." See Landis 1960, 54.

21. The "competitiveness" of markets was never a factor in these price decisions by the commission. See Breyer and MacAvoy 1974.

22. This case is discussed in detail by Kitch 1968. Kitch argues that "the court reasoned from the premise that prices higher than prevailing prices were questionable simply because they were higher" (261). He shows that an examination of the increases that were occurring at the time does not support an argument that this was in response to the producers' demonstrated manipulation of the market.

23. See FPC 1965, vol. 43, p. 15.

24. These and other series described in the next few sentences are from the database used in compiling the econometric gas policy model.

25. An example shows even greater disparities. Wholesale prices charged by the Columbia Gas Transmission Company to the Baltimore retail gas company (Baltimore Gas and Electric) were 43.5 cents per mcf (or per million Btu) in 1970 as a result of frozen field prices, whereas wholesale terminal prices for #2 fuel oil were 86.3 cents per million Btu at the same location that year. Although retail delivery charge could explain part of the difference, it could not explain it all. The size of the difference increased by 30 cents per million Btu per annum in the succeeding three years. The oil and coal price series are from Edison Electric Institute, *Statistical Annual of the Electric Utility Industry* (various years), for these fuels consumed in electric power stations; this is as close to a wholesale price series as can be obtained for comparability with gas sales by pipelines to either retail gas utilities, electric utilities, or other industrial users.

26. See FPC 1972, 36.

27. See ibid., "Initial Rates for Future Gas Sales from All Areas," Docket No. R389A, 42.

28. See FPC 1973, 49.

29. See, e.g., Douglas 1956, esp. 589, where he goes so far as to claim: "Competition in the field is limited by the domination of supply and reserves by a very few companies."

30. *Phillips Petroleum Co. v. Wis.* 347 U.S. 672 (1954) at 685.

31. Southern Louisiana Area Rate Cases (*Austral Oil Co. v. Fed. Power Comm'n*), 428 F.2d 407 (1970) at 416.

32. Hawkins 1969, 32.

33. 34 *FPC* 159 (1956) at 182, n. 17; *Skelly Oil Co. v. Fed. Power Comm'n,* 375 F.2d 6 (10th Cir. 1967); 390 U.S. 747 (1968).

34. Testimony of Professor Adelman before the FPC, *Champlin Oil and Refining Co.,* Docket No. G-9277, 458 L.C., quoted in MacAvoy 1970, 156; McKie 1960, 543.

35. As an example of this argument, see the testimony of Alfred E. Kahn in the Champlin Oil and Refining Company case, FPC Docket No. G-9277.

36. Concentration was higher in the period 1950–1954 in the midcontinent region, given that the four largest producers provided more that two-thirds of new reserves. But the four largest pipelines in this region purchased more than 90 percent of new reserves over this same period. The balance lay with the pipelines because high concentration on the supply side quickly disappeared, with the four largest producers providing only 29 percent in the period 1956–1958 in the same region. See MacAvoy 1962, chs. 5–7.

37. See ibid., ch. 8.

38. On this point, most of the economic theories of the regulated firm agree. The Averch-Johnson theory of the profit-maximizing firm subject to a constraint on rate of return implies no enhancement of the price paid for a noncapital input factor. See Averch and Johnson 1962, 1052–1069; Baumol and Klevorick 1970, 162–190.

39. See MacAvoy 1962.

40. This pattern is found in the first complete area rate decision, *Permian Basin Area Rate Proceeding,* 34 *FPC* 159 (1965), at 160.

41. Much more detail could be provided on the operating practices and regulation of the pipelines before going on to describe the actual performance of wellhead markets. The

pipelines were regulated by the FPC on the basis of the procedures associated with "orthodox" public utility price controls, except on sales to direct industrial consumers or intrastate consumers. Suffice it to say at this point that equations stressing "cost averaging" in the model described in Chapter 2 capture the results from this regulation.

42. The price level that would have cleared production supply and demand has been inserted into the model in order to simulate for 1960–1970 additions to reserves. Reserves are estimated with the equation relationships for discoveries, extensions, and revisions.

43. Demands increased because of the relatively low prices at wholesale following from the earlier frozen field prices. The additions to demands as a result of average pricing can be seen from comparing "production demand" at actual average wholesale prices with the demands that would have been realized at the hypothetical "unregulated" prices in additional simulations of the model. These "artificially induced" additions to demand from the lower frozen prices were of the order of 3 to 4 trillion cubic feet per annum by 1971–1972.

44. This area corresponds to the change in consumer surplus going from the regulatory to the market-clearing scenario. In the absence of regulation, consumer surplus is the large triangular area below the demand curve *but* above the market-clearing price. In the historical or regulated scenario, the consumer surplus is the area below the demand curve and above the regulated price, truncated by the limited historical supply. The difference in area is triangle *A* and triangle *B* (fig. 3.3).

This approach is also used to calculate the gains and losses of producers. Producer surplus is the area above the supply curve but below the market or regulated price. The change in this area, which is the loss in producer surplus with regulation, is the total of areas *A* and *C.*

45. 15 U.S.C.A. §§ 3301–3432 (Supp. 1979).

46. "Lingering Death" 1975, 5.

47. Bethell 1979, 105.

48. U.S. Senate 1998, 68.

49. Ibid., 92.

50. 15 U.S.C.A. § 3312 (Supp. 1979).

51. Ibid., § 3331.

52. Ibid., § 3312(c)(1)(B).

53. Ibid. §§ 3341, 3343.

54. Ibid. Also included were the higher prices for gas from new liquefied natural gas (LNG) projects. The price increments for North Slope Alaskan gas, for manufactured or synthetic natural gas (SNG), and for currently approved LNG projects would be "rolled in" existing wholesale rates.

55. 15 U.S.C.A. § 3344 (Supp. 1979). This industrial gas price ceiling was supposed to vary by geographic region, since it was to be based on distillate and residual fuel prices at specific locations. Those specifications made the choice of the comparable fuel oil price important for achieving price deregulation. Using the higher distillate price would shift less of gas field price increases to residential consumers and more to industrial customers.

56. DOE 1979; DOE/EIA 1978.

57. See Russell 1983, 21.

58. Carpenter, Jacoby, and Wright 1988.

59. See *Northern Natural Gas Co.*, 16 *FERC* 61,109 at 61,244 (July 31, 1981).

60. See DOE/EIA 1983.

61. In addition, given price controls on old contract gas, the interstate pipelines expanded availability from locked-in sources by offering "take-or-pay" agreements and "price renegotiation" on production in future years. In one analysis of these provision the DOE/EIA described 1980 to 1982 as that period in which the interstate pipelines aggressively offered non-price terms favorable to producers on production scheduling and payment schedules. See DOE/EIA 1987, 34. This report examines contracts for gas flowing under the NGPA Sections 102, 103, 107, and 108 (defined as "new" gas from the post-NGPA wells). The principle data source for this study was a stratified random sample of 1,096 post-NGPA wells conducted in 1985. The DOE/EIA describes this survey as the only comprehensive source of information on contract provisions in effect during 1982–1985.

62. See DOE/EIA 1990, table 29.

63. See DOE/EIA 1989, 16. See also Doane and Spulber 1994.

64. See FERC, Notice of Proposed Rule Making, Pipeline Service Obligations and Revisions to Regulations Governing Self-Implementing Transportation Under Part 284 of the Commission Regulations, Docket No. RM91-11-000, 56 Fed. Reg. 38,372 (1991).

CHAPTER 4: THE PARTIAL DEREGULATION OF TRANSPORTATION AND THE CREATION OF A SINGLE NORTH AMERICAN GAS MARKET

1. FERC Order No. 436, Regulation of Natural Gas Pipelines After Partial Wellhead Decontrol, FERC Stats. & Regs., ¶ 30,665 et seq. (1985), and, as amended, FERC Stats. & Regs., ¶ 30,675 (1985).

2. FERC Order No. 519, Limitation on Incentive Prices for High Cost Gas to Commodity Values, FERC Stats. & Regs. ¶ 30–879 (1990). See also FERC Order No. 523, Order Implementing the Natural Gas Wellhead Decontrol Act of 1989, FERC Stats. & Regs., ¶ 30,887 (1990).

3. C.F.R. 18 §§ 284.221, 284.223 (1986).

4. See FERC, Request for Comments on Alternative Pricing Methods, Docket No. RM95-6-00, 70 FERC ¶ 61,139; and FERC, Policy Statement and Request for Comments, Docket No. RM96-7-00, 74 FERC ¶ 61,076.

5. See DOE/EIA, Office of Oil and Gas 1998, 94, fig. 32: Reserved, Utilized, and Available Capacity for the 1996–97 Heating Year.

6. See FERC Order No. 636 (Apr. 8, 1992), 61 FERC 61,030; FERC Order No. 636-A (Aug. 3, 1992), 61 FERC 61,102; and FERC Order No. 636-B (Nov. 27, 1992), 61 FERC 61,272; all in 19 C.F.R. Part 284.

7. FERC, Notice of Proposed Rule Making, Pipeline Service Obligations and Revisions to Regulations Governing Self-Implementing Transportation Under Part 284 of the Commission Regulations, Docket No. RM91-11-000 (July 31, 1991), 56 Fed. Reg. 38,372.

8. See FERC Order No. 636 at 7.

9. Ibid., quoting from H.R. Rep. No. 29, 101st Cong., 1st Sess. 2 (1989).

10. Tirole 1988, ch. 5.

11. This relationship in the specific case of noncollusive quantity (or capacity) determination by each pipeline can be formulated as follows. The determinants of the transportation rate are (1) the marginal cost of transportation, (2) the number of equivalent-sized pipelines, and (3) the elasticity of two-city market demand for transportation services. The two-city price difference $[P_d - P_u]$ is in equilibrium for each firm when $(P_d - P_u) = MC/[1 + HHI/e]$, where P_d = gas price at the downstream city gate; P_u = gas price at the upstream market center; MC = marginal cost of transportation from the market center to the city gate; HHI = Herfindahl-Hirschman Index; and e = elasticity of demand for transportation. Thus, the gas price difference, equal to the actual transportation rate, will be higher as MC and the HHI increase and will be lower as the elasticity of demand becomes larger.

12. Market hubs are located either in producing regions near the intersection of several pipelines or in consuming regions near large storage fields. In the early 1990s, according to the commission, there were thirteen market hubs in the continental United States; Blanco, N.Mex.; Detroit, Mich.; Erath, La.; Guymon, Okla.; Katy, Tex.; Lebanon, Ohio; Leidy, Pa.; Midland–Waha, Tex.; Monroe, La.; Niagara, N.Y.; Opal, Wyo.; Topock, Ariz.; and Tucola, Ill. See Federal Energy Regulatory Commission, Office of Economic Policy 1991.

13. HHI equals Σs_i^2, the sum of the squares of firm market shares i.

14. The exception being Katy, Tex., to New York City and Monroe, La., to New York City, two separate pairs combined to form one city-pair, given that Lebanon, Ohio, is an intermediate point between supply sources in Texas and demand sources in the New York region.

15. Using this method a variable Z is transformed to $Z(\lambda - 1)/\lambda$. Since the limit of this as λ approaches zero is ln Z, it is defined to be Z when $\lambda = 0$. If all variables in a linear functional form are transformed this way and λ is estimated (in conjunction with the other variables using maximum likelihood estimation), significance tests can be performed to check the special cases of λ. For example, if $\lambda = 0$, the functional form is log-linear; if $\lambda = 1$, it is linear. See Box and Cox 1964; and Seaks and Laysen 1983.

16. A variant of the competitiveness hypothesis focuses on seasonal competition only. Suppose, for the sake of argument, that a pipeline was able to exercise market power in peak heating periods but not during other periods, when carriers have excess capacity. This pipeline would not have to discount tariffs rates in the winter, so that winter gas price differences would be larger than those in other seasons ($b_6 > 0$).

17. As indicated by the t-statistics, shown in parentheses, exceeding absolute values of 2.

18. Interstate Natural Gas Association of America 1996.

19. See Simpson 1994.

20. See DOE/EIA 1994.

CHAPTER 5: THE UNBUNDLING OF LOCAL GAS RETAIL MARKETS

1. DOE/EIA, Gas and Oil Division 2000.

2. With the exception that the federal Department of Transportation retains ultimate responsibility for regulations related to pipeline safety.

3. Under PG&E's Gas Accord, the California Public Utilities Commission has authorized an unbundled rate structure for PG&E's extensive high-pressure backbone system, similar to an intrastate pipeline structure. However, the utility is regulated in California as a local distribution company.

CHAPTER 6: PARTIAL DEREGULATION AND THE FUTURE PERFORMANCE OF GAS MARKETS

1. There were difficulties in applying this procedure with one equation, that for the change in the price of petroleum (with R-square of 13.5 percent of the equation variance, leaving a large variance for ϵ relative to the value of the dependent variable). In order to avoid negative values for this price, a regression error of zero was assigned for all years.

References

"AGA Cites 78% Gas Replacement Rate by Majors." 1986. *Oil and Gas Journal,* May 26, 39.

American Gas Association (AGA). 1977. *Offshore Gas and Oil Supply Model.* Arlington, Va.: American Gas Association.

———. 1978. *Offshore Gas and Oil Supply Model.* Arlington, Va.: American Gas Association.

———. 1979. *Offshore Gas and Oil Supply Model.* Arlington, Va.: American Gas Association.

———. *Gas Energy Review* (suppl.).

Averch, Harvey, and Leland L. Johnson. 1962. "Behavior of the Firm Under Regulatory Constraint." *American Economic Review* 52, no. 1 (December): 1052–1096.

"Bankers Trust Urges Gas Drilling Hike." 1984. *Oil and Gas Journal,* Sept. 24, 40.

Baumol, William J., and Alvin K. Klevorick. 1970. "Input Choices and Rate-of-Return Regulation: An Overview of the Discussion." *Bell Journal of Economics and Management Science* 1 (Autumn): 162–190.

Berndt, Ernst R. 1991. *The Practice of Econometrics.* Reading, Mass.: Addison-Wesley.

Bethell, Tom. 1979. "The Gas Price Fixers." *Harper's,* June, 37–44.

Box, G., and R. Cox. 1964."Analysis of Transformations." *Journal of the Royal Statistical Society* 26, ser. B (April): 211–243.

Breyer, Stephen G., and Paul W. MacAvoy. 1973. "The Natural Gas Shortage and Regulation of Natural Gas Producers." *Harvard Law Review* 86, no. 3:941–987.

———. 1974. *Energy Regulation by the Federal Power Commission.* Washington, D.C.: Brookings Institution.

Bureau of Budget. 1970. *The Budget of the United States Government—Appendix, Fiscal Year 1970.* Washington, D.C.: U.S. Government Printing Office.

Carpenter, P. R., H. D. Jacoby, and A. W. Wright. 1988. "Adapting to Change in Natural Gas Markets." In *Energy: Markets and Regulation—Essays in Honor of M. A. Adelman,* 1–29. Edited by R. L. Gordon et al. Cambridge, Mass.: MIT Press.

"Change, Uncertainty Mark U.S. Natural-Gas Market." 1988. *Oil and Gas Journal,* June 6, 42.

"Chase Manhattan: Gas Surplus Will End in 1985." 1984. *Oil and Gas Journal,* June 25, 51.

Cushman, Robert E. 1941. *The Independent Regulatory Commissions.* Oxford: Oxford University Press.

Doane, Michael J., and Daniel F. Spulber. 1994. "Open Access and the Evolution of the U.S. Spot Market for Natural Gas." *Journal of Law and Economics* 37, no. 2 (October): 477–517.

Douglas, Paul H. 1956. "The Case for the Consumer of Natural Gas." *Georgetown Law Journal* 44 (June): 566–606.

Durbin, J. 1970. "Testing for Serial Correlation in Least Squares Regression When Some of the Regressors Are Lagged Dependent Variables." *Econometrica* 38:410–421.

Edison Electric Institute. *Statistical Annual of the Electric Utility Industry.* Washington, D.C.: Edison Electric Institute. (Various years.)

Executive Office of the President. 1992. *Economic Report of the President.* Washington, D.C.: U.S. Government Printing Office.

Federal Energy Regulatory Commission (FERC). Office of Economic Policy. 1991. *Importance of Market Centers.* Washington, D.C.: U.S. Government Printing Office.

Foster Associates. 1979–1981. "Foster Bulletin on Regulated Gas." (Various editions.)

Gallick, E. G. 1993. *Competition in the Natural Gas Industry: An Economic Policy Analysis.* Westport, Conn.: Praeger.

Gas Research Institute. 1988. "Gas Supplies Will Tighten in the 1990s, But Will Meet Demand." *Industrial Energy Bulletin,* June 8.

Gerwig, Robert W. 1962. "Natural Gas Production: A Study of Costs of Regulation." *Journal of Law and Economics* 5 (October): 69–92.

Hatanaka, Michio. 1974. "An Efficient Estimator for the Dynamic Adjustment Model with Auto-Correlated Errors." *Journal of Econometrics* 2:199–220.

Hawkins, Clark A. 1969. *The Field Price Regulation of Natural Gas.* Tallahassee: Florida State University Press.

Hotelling, Harold. 1931. "The Economics of Exhaustible Resources." *Journal of Political Economy* 39, no. 2 (April): 137–175.

Interstate Natural Gas Association of America. 1996. *Gas Transportation Through the First Half of 1995.* Report No. 96-1. Washington, D.C.: Interstate Natural Gas Association of America (February).

Kitch, Edmund W. 1968. "Regulation of the Field Market for Natural Gas by the Federal Power Commission." *Journal of Law and Economics* 11 (October): 243–280.

Landis, James M. 1960. *Report on Regulatory Agencies to the President-Elect.* Subcommittee on Administrative Practice and Procedure of the U.S. Senate Committee on the Judiciary. 85th Cong., 2d Sess. Washington, D.C.: U.S. Government Printing Office (December).

"A Lingering Death." 1975. *New Republic,* June 10, 5.

MacAvoy, Paul W. 1962. *Price Formation in Natural Gas Fields: A Study of Competition, Monopsony, and Regulation.* New Haven: Yale University Press.

———. 1965. *The Economics Effects of Regulation: Trunk-Line Railroad Cartels and Interstate Commerce Commission, 1870–1900.* Cambridge, Mass.: MIT Press.

———. 1970. *The Crisis of the Regulatory Commissions.* New York: W. W. Norton.

———. 1983. *Energy Policy: An Economic Analysis.* New York: W. W. Norton.

———. 1994. "Prices After Deregulation: The United States Experience." *Hume Papers on Public Policy* 1, no. 3 (January): 45.

McKie, James W. 1960. "Market Structure and Uncertainty in Oil and Gas Exploration." *Quarterly Journal of Economics* 74 (November): 543–571.

Mulherin, J. Harold. 1986. "Complexity in Long-Term Contracts: An Analysis of Natural Gas Contractual Provisions." *Journal of Law, Economics and Organization* 2, no. 1:105–117.

"OGJ Newsletter." 1985. *Oil and Gas Journal,* Sept. 2, 5.

Pierce, Jr., Richard J., and Ernest Gellhorn. 1994. *Regulated Industries in a Nutshell.* St. Paul, Minn.: West.

Pindyck, Robert S. 1978. "The Optimal Exploration and Production of Nonrenewable Resources." *Journal of Political Economy* 86, no. 5:841–861.

Potential Gas Committee. 1971. *Potential Supply of Natural Gas in the United States.* Boulder: Colorado University, Mineral Resources Institute, Potential Gas Association.

———. 1973. *Potential Supply of Natural Gas in the United States.* Boulder: Colorado University, Mineral Resources Institute, Potential Gas Association.

President's Advisory Council on Executive Organization. 1971. *A New Regulatory Framework: Report on Selected Independent Regulatory Agencies.* Washington, D.C.: U.S. Government Printing Office.

Russell, Milton. 1983. "Overview of Policy Issues: A Preliminary Assessment." In *The Deregulation of Natural Gas,* 3–32. Edited by Edward J. Mitchell. Washington, D.C.: American Enterprise Institute for Public Policy Research.

Seaks, T. G., and S. K. Laysen. 1983. "Box-Cox Estimation with Standard Econometric Problems." *Review of Economics and Statistics* 65, no. 1:160–164.

Simpson, J. "Restructured Industry Weathers First Test." 1994. *Public Utilities Fortnightly,* April 1, 34–35.

Tirole, Jean. 1988. *The Theory of Industrial Organization.* Cambridge, Mass.: MIT Press.

Tussing, Arlon, and Bob Tippee, with Connie C. Barlow. 1995. *The Natural Gas Industry: Evolution, Structure and Economics,* 2d ed. Tulsa, Okla.: Pennwell Books.

U.S. Department of Energy (DOE). 1979. *Energy Supply and Demand in the Mid-Term: 1985–1990, and 1995.* Washington, D.C.: U.S. Government Printing Office.

U.S. Department of Energy, Energy Information Administration (DOE/EIA). 1978. *An Evaluation of Natural Gas Pricing Proposals*. Washington, D.C.: U.S. Government Printing Office.

―――. 1980–1990. *State Energy Price and Expenditure Report*. DOE/EIA-0376. Washington, D.C.: U.S. Government Printing Office. (Various years.)

―――. 1983. *Structure and Trends in Natural Gas Wellhead Contracts*. Washington, D.C.: U.S. Government Printing Office, November.

―――. 1987. *An Analysis of Natural Gas Contracts*. Vol. 2: *Contract Provisions Covering Production of New Gas*. DOE/EIA-0505. Washington, D.C.: U.S. Government Printing Office.

―――. 1988. *Annual Energy Outlook, 1988*. Washington, D.C.: U.S. Government Printing Office.

―――. 1989. *Growth in Unbundled Natural Gas Transportation Services: 1982–1987*. DOE/EIA-0525. Washington, D.C.: U.S. Government Printing Office.

―――. 1990. *Annual Energy Review, 1990*. DOE/EIA-0131. Washington, D.C.: U.S. Government Printing Office.

―――. 1994. *Natural Gas, 1994: Issues and Trends*. DOE/EIA-0560. Washington, D.C.: U.S. Government Printing Office.

―――. 1996. *Annual Energy Review, 1996*. DOE/EIA-0384. Washington, D.C.: U.S. Government Printing Office.

U.S. Department of Energy. Energy Information Administration (DOE/EIA). Gas and Oil Division. 2000. *Status of Natural Gas Residential Choice Programs by State as of March 2000*. Washington, D.C.: U.S. Government Printing Office.

U.S. Department of Energy. Energy Information Administration (DOE/EIA). Office of Oil and Gas. 1998. *Deliverability on the Interstate Natural Gas Pipeline System*. DOE/EIA-0618. Washington, D.C.: U.S. Government Printing Office, May.

U.S. Department of Justice. 1986. *Report of Oil Pipeline Deregulation*. Washington, D.C.: U.S. Government Printing Office, May.

U.S. Department of the Interior. National Petroleum Council. 1971 (interim report) / 1972 (final report). *U.S. Energy Outlook: Oil and Gas Availability*. Washington, D.C.: U.S. Government Printing Office.

U.S. Department of the Interior. U.S. Geological Survey. 1973. "U.S. Mineral Resources," Circular 650. Washington, D.C.: U.S. Government Printing Office.

U.S. Federal Power Commission (FPC). 1956. *Annual Report for 1955*. Washington, D.C.: U.S. Government Printing Office.

―――. 1965. *Annual Report for 1964*. Washington, D.C.: U.S. Government Printing Office, 43.

―――. 1969. *Annual Report for 1968*. Washington, D.C.: U.S. Government Printing Office.

―――. 1970. *Annual Report for 1969*. Washington, D.C.: U.S. Government Printing Office.

―――. 1971. *Statistics of Interstate Natural Gas Pipeline Companies, 1970*.

―――. 1972. *Annual Report for 1971*. Washington, D.C.: U.S. Government Printing Office.

―――. 1973. *Annual Report for 1972*. Washington, D.C.: U.S. Government Printing Office.

―――. *Statistics of Natural Gas Pipelines*. (Annual; various years.)

U.S. Federal Power Commission (FPC). Bureau of Natural Gas. 1972. *National Case Supply and Demand, 1971–1990.* Washington, D.C.: U.S. Government Printing Office, February.

U.S. Government Accounting Office. 1998. *Energy Deregulation: Status of Natural Gas Customer Choice Programs.* GAO/RCED 99-30, Dec. 15.

U.S. Senate. 1998. *The Conference Report on Natural Gas.* Joint Explanatory Statement of the Committee on Conference, S. Rep. 95-1126, 95th Cong., 2d Sess., 68.

"Weak Wellhead Prices Fail to Bolster Recovery in U.S. Gas Well Drilling." 1989. *Oil and Gas Journal,* Feb. 6, 15.

Index